Contemporary Studies in Literature

Eugene Ehrlich, *Columbia University*
Daniel Murphy, *City University of New York*
Series Editors

Volumes include:

T. S. ELIOT, edited by Linda Wagner

WILLIAM FAULKNER, edited by
Dean M. Schmitter

F. SCOTT FITZGERALD, edited by
Kenneth E. Eble

ERNEST HEMINGWAY, edited by
Arthur Waldhorn

JAMES JOYCE, edited by
Chester G. Anderson

FRANZ KAFKA, edited by Leo Hamalian

D. H. LAWRENCE, edited by Leo Hamalian

EZRA POUND, edited by Grace Schulman

MARK TWAIN, edited by Dean M. Schmitter

WALT WHITMAN, edited by Arthur Golden

W. B. YEATS, edited by Patrick J. Keane

Walt
Whitman

a collection of criticism edited by Arthur Golden

McGraw-Hill Book Company

New York • St. Louis • San Francisco • London • Düsseldorf

Kuala Lumpur • Mexico • Montreal • Panama • São Paulo

Sydney • Toronto • Johannesburg • New Delhi • Singapore

to my mother and to the memory of my father

123456789MUMU7987654

Library of Congress Cataloging in Publication Data

Golden, Arthur, comp.

Walt Whitman; a collection of criticism.

(Contemporary studies in literature)
Bibliography: p.
1. Whitman, Walt, 1819–1892
PS3238.G6   811'.3   73-14670
ISBN 0–070–23656–9

Preface

This collection of essays covers from a variety of critical approaches the wide range of Whitman's poetry, the influences that shaped his sensibility, and his own strong influence on the direction of modern poetry.

Over a thirty-seven year period, Whitman had published six separate editions of *Leaves of Grass*. In the process he also labored to create a distinct public personality—with an assist from his followers—that until only recently tended to shift attention away from, if not at times overshadow, his achievements as a poet. In the Introduction, I discuss the growth of *Leaves of Grass* and attempt to separate the serious artist from the public relations image.

In Part I, "The Long Foreground," Gay Wilson Allen surveys Whitman's preparation for the writing of the poems of the first edition of *Leaves*. Professor Allen clears up much of the nonsense written about the so-called miracle of the transformation of a hack journalist into a great poet.

In Part II, "The Creative Process," G. W. Allen discusses several meaningful critical approaches to the various editions of *Leaves of Grass;* Roger Asselineau traces Whitman's gradual shift from the innovative language of his early poetry to a more traditional approach in his later work; and Stanley K. Coffman, Jr., in his analysis of the poem "Crossing Brooklyn Ferry," discusses Whitman's important "catalogue" technique. Edwin H. Miller and Stephen E. Whicher offer close readings of "There Was a Child Went Forth" and "Out of the Cradle Endlessly Rocking," and James E. Miller, Jr., assesses Whitman's influence on, among others, such poets as Dylan Thomas, Garcia Lorca, Hart Crane, and Allen Ginsberg.

Part III, "The Revisory Process," consists of a discussion of the impact of the Civil War on Whitman's poetry and the way in which he shaped *Leaves of Grass* for future editions through extensive and important revisions in his personal copy of the third edition.

In the final part, "Democratic Vistas," Richard Chase presents a close analysis of Whitman's commitment to the democratic ideal.

Quotations from the various editions of *Leaves of Grass* cited in these essays have been checked and, where necessary, silently corrected.

A. G.

The City College of the City University of New York, June 1973

v

Contents

Chronology

1819	*Born May 31 at West Hills, Long Island.*
1823	*Family moves to Brooklyn.*
1825–30	*Attends school in Brooklyn.*
1830–42	*Apprentice printer; teaches school on Long Island; founds* Long-Islander *newspaper (still being published in Huntington, Long Island); edits and contributes to various journals; publishes temperance novel* Franklin Evans, or the Inebriate *(1842).*
1845–46	*Continues journalism.*
1846–48	*Edits Brooklyn* Daily Eagle *and discharged by owner over political differences; in early 1848 goes to New Orleans to work on* Crescent; *leaves in May.*
1848–49	*Edits Brooklyn* Freeman, *a "free-soil" newspaper.*
1850–54	*Operates a printing office; does freelance journalism; builds houses; speculates in real estate.*
1855	*First edition,* Leaves of Grass; *Emerson writes famous letter, greeting Whitman "at the beginning of a great career."*
1856	*Second edition,* Leaves of Grass; *begins practice of adding new poems to* Leaves, *while revising those published in earlier editions.*
1857–59	*Edits Brooklyn* Daily Times.
1860	*Third edition,* Leaves of Grass.
1862–64	*Visits Fredericksburg, Virginia, in search of brother George, in Union Army, reported wounded in action; works part-time in Army Paymaster's Office in Washington, D.C.; serves as volunteer aide in Army hospitals in Washington; contracts "hospital malaria" and returns to Brooklyn in June 1864 to recuperate; by September 1864, health "quite re-established."*
1865	*In January obtains clerk's position in Indian Bureau of the Department of the Interior;* Drum-Taps *pub-*

lished; in June fired by Secretary of the Interior James Harlan who was scandalized by Leaves of Grass; *hired next day as clerk in Attorney General's Office at intercession of influential friend;* Sequel to Drum-Taps *published.*

1866 *William D. O'Connor publishes vigorous defense of Whitman,* The Good Gray Poet: A Vindication.

1867 *Fourth edition,* Leaves of Grass.

1871 *Fifth edition,* Leaves of Grass; Passage to India; Democratic Vistas.

1873 *Suffers paralytic stroke, leaves Washington to take up residence in Camden, New Jersey.*

1876 *Centennial edition* Leaves of Grass *(reprint of Fifth edition) and companion volume* Two Rivulets.

1879–80 *Trip to Colorado; St. Louis; and London, Ontario.*

1881 *Sixth edition,* Leaves of Grass, *in which Whitman settles on the final arrangement of poems. Published in Boston, where District Attorney threatens prosecution unless* Leaves *withdrawn from mails or expurgated; Whitman refuses and* Leaves *published intact by Philadelphia house in 1882, also date for* Specimen Days.

1888 November Boughs.

1891 Good-Bye My Fancy.

1891–92 *Final, "Deathbed" edition of* Leaves of Grass.

1892 *Dies March 26 in Camden, New Jersey; buried in Harleigh Cemetery, Camden.*

Arthur Golden

Introduction

Whitman has managed to survive his disciples and detractors. Whitman as poet has finally been untangled from Whitman as public personality, Whitman as purveyor of public-relations charades, and Whitman as dirty poet who took it upon himself to liberate the sexuality of a repressed American public. Given the kind of poetry he wrote and the genteel age in which he published his work, the fierce loyalties and antagonisms that he generated are understandable. Unfortunately, for many years they had the effect of shifting attention away from the poetry itself to the personality of the poet and the battles fought around him.

Whitman was hardly calculated to endear himself to a mid-nineteenth-century public comfortable with traditional verses evoking the dignity of European byways and exotic virginal romances, verses in a predictable meter that soothed the respectable and instructed them gently in matters of moral rectitude and the justness of homely virtues. American poets of the time had leaned rather heavily on the literary traditions of England, but the intensely nationalistic Whitman would not. He had soaked up what Emerson and others had been saying about the need for, and the requirements of, a distinctly American poet. (Whitman has said that he was "simmering, simmering, simmering" and Emerson brought him to a boil.) Quite simply, and in all details and specifications, he was that poet.

In his essay "The Poet," Emerson wrote:

> For the experience of each new age requires a new confession, and the world seems always waiting for its poet. . . .

1

The vocabulary of an omniscient man would embrace words and images excluded from polite conversation. What would be base, or even obscene, to the obscene, becomes illustrious, spoken in a new connection of thought. . . .

The poet knows that he speaks adequately . . . only when he speaks somewhat wildly, or "with the flower of the mind"; not with the intellect used as an organ, but with the intellect released from all services and suffered to take its direction from its celestial life; or as the ancients were wont to express themselves, not with the intellect alone but with the intellect inebriated by nectar. . . .

We do not with sufficient plainness or sufficient profoundness address ourselves to life, nor dare we chaunt our own times and social circumstance. . . . We have yet had no genius in America, with tyrannous eye, which knew the value of our incomparable materials, and saw, in the barbarism and materialism of the times, another carnival of the same gods whose picture he so much admires in Homer; then in the Middle Age; then in Calvinism. Banks and tariffs, the newspaper and caucus, Methodism and Unitarianism, are flat and dull to dull people, but rest on the same foundations of wonder as the town of Troy and the temple of Delphi, and are as swiftly passing away. Our log-rolling, our stumps and their politics, our fisheries, our Negroes and Indians, our boats and our repudiations, the wrath of rogues and the pusillanimity of honest men, the northern trade, the southern planting, the western clearing, Oregon and Texas, are yet unsung. Yet America is a poem in our eyes; its ample geography dazzles the imagination, and it will not long wait for meters.

Whitman said, "The Americans of all nations at any time upon the earth have probably the fullest poetical nature. The United States themselves are essentially the greatest poem." He preferred the "blab," the excitement of his native Manhattan and Brooklyn streets to spired cathedral cities out of books. Romance was a return to a Garden of Eden innocence in sexual matters, conveyed in explicit, colloquial American English. Middle-class respectability blocked American men and women from coming together on terms of perfect equality, from openly and honestly coming to grips with their true selves and natural appetites. Whitman, "an American, one of the roughs, a kosmos," was the self-proclaimed enlightened Everyman with the gift of song.

Whitman's voice was that of the prophet, bard, seer, his style that of the Bible. He wrote in two- and three-line units, with the second and third lines generally supporting, adding to, or contradicting the first. He wrote in free verse, that is, poetry of irregular meter and without rhyme. He relied heavily on the rhythms of native American speech. He said "I am the poet of the body, / And I am the poet of the soul," but at the beginning of his career, at any rate, he spent most of his time on the body.

> Urge and urge and urge,
> Always the procreant urge of the world.

> Out of the dimness opposite equals advance . . . . Always
>   substance and increase,
> Always a knit of identity . . . . always distinction . . . .
>   always a breed of life.[1]

> I am the poet of the woman the same as the man,
> And I say it is as great to be a woman as to be a man,
> And I say there is nothing greater than the mother of men.

> I chant a new chant of dilation or pride,
> We have had ducking and deprecating about enough,
> I show that size is only developement.

> Who need be afraid of the merge?
> Undrape . . . . you are not guilty to me, nor stale nor
>   discarded,
> I see through the broadcloth and gingham whether or no,
> And am around, tenacious, acquisitive, tireless . . . . and
>   can never be shaken away.

> On women fit for conception I start bigger and nimbler babes,
> This day I am jetting the stuff of far more arrogant republics.

His muses were his contemporaries, no matter what their station in society:

> The hounded slave that flags in the race and leans by the
>   fence, blowing and covered with sweat,

---

[1] In the first (1855) edition of *Leaves of Grass,* Whitman relied heavily on four spaced periods to mark a rhythmical break within the line. He abandoned this device thereafter, using instead conventional punctuation.

The twinges that sting like needles his legs and neck,
The murderous buckshot and the bullets,
All these I feel or am.

I am the hounded slave . . . . I wince at the bite of the dogs,
Hell and despair are upon me . . . . crack and again crack the
    marksmen,
I clutch the rails of the fence . . . . my gore dribs thin with
    the ooze of my skin,
I fall on the weeds and stones,
The riders spur their unwilling horses and haul close,
They taunt my dizzy ears . . . . they beat me violently over the
    head with their whip-stocks.

Agonies are one of my changes of garments;
I do not ask the wounded person how he feels . . . . I myself
    become the wounded person,
My hurt turns livid upon me as I lean on a cane and observe.

He identified with the mechanic, athlete, Indian, trapper, half-breed, bus driver, and, for good measure, the emptier of privies, the prostitute, and the "venerealee." These were his "camera-does."

He exalted the commonplace. "I believe a leaf of grass is no less than the journeywork of the stars, / And the pismire is equally perfect, and a grain of sand, and the egg of a wren" and "A morning-glory at my window satisfies me more than the metaphysics of books." He got off some funny lines at a time when writing poetry in America was a self-consciously lofty and serious business. "Who goes there! hankering, gross, mystical, nude? / How is it I extract strength from the beef I eat?" And he gave his enemies a good opening with "I sound my barbaric yawp over the roofs of the world."

He said, "I do not despise you priests." But while he did not actually despise priests, he did not like them either. To Whitman the priest was any representative of an institutionalized religion predicated on the "thou shalt not" syndrome, exactly the kind of minister that Emerson had upended in his "Divinity School Address" in 1838. As Whitman saw it, "Logic and sermons never convince, / The damp of the night drives deeper into my soul" and "Divine am I inside and out, and I make holy whatever I touch or am touched from; / The scent of these arm-pits is aroma finer than prayer, / This head is more than churches or bibles or creeds." All this from "Song of Myself," the opening poem of the revolutionary first edition of *Leaves of Grass*.[2] There was more of the same in several of the other eleven poems that made up the first edition, namely "The Sleepers," that "fantasia of the unconscious," in Malcolm Cowley's apt phrase, and "I Sing the Body Electric." The first edition also contained the masterfully controlled poem of a child's initiation into the adult world, "There Was A Child Went Forth."

This slim quarto volume *Leaves of Grass,* ornately bound and printed at Whitman's expense (only a few of the later editions were brought out by publishers), also featured a portrait of the soft-spoken Whitman disguised as his persona, the resonant bardic poet. The reader opened to a casual, supremely self-confident Whitman, sporting a rakish Spanish hat atop a head cocked to one side, his beard carefully trimmed, his undershirt defiantly in view beneath an open collar, one hand on his hip, the other casually in the pocket of his workman's pants. Following the portrait, and coming right before "Song of Myself," there was a rambling, galvanic preface. With its bravado, its extravagance of rhetoric, and its explosive confidence, it was exactly the right sounding board for the daring poetry it introduced. The author's name was coyly missing from the title page but included on the reverse copyright page as "Walter Whitman" and in "Song of Myself" as the more appropriately bardic "Walt Whitman."

With all this Whitman turned out to be a prophet whose liberating message proved too strong to attract an instant following. The first edition did not sell. One infidel set the tone for what was to become a more or less predictable commentary on Whitman's poetry for years to come: "As to the volume itself, we have only to remark, that it strongly fortifies the doctrines of the Metempsychosists, for it is impossible to imagine how any man's fancy could have conceived such a mass of stupid filth, unless he were possessed of the soul of a sentimental donkey that had died of disappointed love. This *poet (?)* without wit, but with a certain vagrant wildness, just serves to show the energy which natural imbecility is occasionally capable of under strong excitement." (In later years another reviewer simplified matters by suggesting that Whitman ought to kill himself.)

Whitman wished to set the record straight on the merits of *Leaves of Grass.* He therefore wrote three highly complimentary reviews of the first edition, one of which actually included the

---

[2] The poems of the first edition were untitled. In subsequent editions Whitman added titles, often changing the title of the same poem from edition to edition. Only final titles (i.e., from the 1891–92 edition) are cited in the Introduction.

results of a meticulous examination of his cranial topography performed by a well-known phrenologist who also doubled as distributor of the first edition in his Broadway bookshop. (The phrenologist saw great things in the contours of the bumps on Whitman's head.) Whitman took the understandable precaution of publishing these reviews anonymously in various newspapers.

Apparently in order to get the sales moving, he bound into some remaining copies of the first edition eight pages of reviews and carefully selected prose excerpts to give *Leaves* the appearance of a long-awaited work that had finally arrived. His own three unsigned reviews were there, along with others negative in various degrees. The point of all this was obvious. There were perceptive reviewers around who were able to recognize the worth of a great though unconventional poet when he first appeared, as well as dull clods who were not.

From what we know of Whitman's debt to Emerson, it was hardly accidental that he had sent Emerson, whom he had not yet met personally, a complimentary copy of the first edition. Emerson had said back in the 1840's that he looked "in vain for the poet whom I describe." He looked no further. His famous letter is worth quoting in full.

Concord 21 July
Mass^{tts} 1855

Dear   Sir,

      I am not blind to the worth of the wonderful gift of "Leaves of Grass." I find it the most extraordinary piece of wit & wisdom that America has yet contributed. I am very happy in reading it, as great power makes us happy. It meets the demand I am always making of what seemed the sterile & stingy nature, as if too much handiwork or too much lymph in the temperament were making our western wits fat & mean.

      I give you joy of your free & brave thought. I have great joy in it. I find incomparable things said incomparably well, as they must be. I find the courage of *treatment,* which so delights us, & which large perception only can inspire.

      I greet you at the beginning of a great career, which yet must have had a long foreground somewhere, for such a start. I rubbed my eyes a little to see if this sunbeam were no illusion; but the solid sense of the book is a sober certainty. It has the best merits, namely, of fortifying & encouraging.

      I did not know until I, last night, saw the book advertised in a newspaper, that I could trust the name as real & available for a post-

office. I wish to see my benefactor, & have felt much like striking my
tasks, & visiting New York to pay you my respects.

R. W. Emerson.

Mr. Walter Whitman.

In short, in one stroke Whitman had turned around the whole
direction of American poetry, although it was not until after his
death that the full impact of his poetic revolution was felt in the
works of such poets as Ezra Pound, William Carlos Williams, Carl
Sandburg, Wallace Stevens, Louis Simpson, Allen Ginsberg, and
others.

Without permission, Whitman proceeded a few months later
to print Emerson's letter in the New York *Herald.* A few months
later, still without permission, he had the key words of the letter,
"I Greet You at the Beginning of A Great Career R. W.
Emerson." stamped in gold on the spine of the second (1856)
edition, which Emerson had not seen. (Emerson soon forgave this
indiscretion.) The second edition included the original twelve
poems and twenty new ones. Among this latter group was one of
his masterpieces, "Crossing Brooklyn Ferry," the strongly nationalistic "Song of the Broad-Axe," "Salut au Monde!" and the two
well-known poems celebrating physical love, "A Woman Waits for
Me" and "Spontaneous Me."

Whitman continued in the second edition his strenuous
attempt to create a significant public personality. He included the
"Camerado" portrait of the first edition, the mixed-reviews dodge
(with one of his own reviews charitably dropped along the way), as
well as a rambling and euphoric twelve-page open letter to
Emerson. With all this, the second edition did not cause a stir.

It was in the 1856 edition also that Whitman started his practice of revising poems already in print, while he added new poems
to *Leaves of Grass,* which in turn underwent subsequent revision.
Apparently his penchant for public-relations monkeyshines was
one side of his complex personality, one that antagonistic
critics have stressed, while generally shying away from attempting a balanced assessment of the range, imaginativeness, and
variety of the poetry itself. In this respect, Whitman was his own
worst enemy, as he was soon to realize. The point is that Whitman
was a hard-working, meticulous craftsman who carefully revised
his poetry over the years as he tried to bring it closely into
line with his own growth and development. His revisions ranged
from a continual probing for the exact word or phrase to the alteration or deletion of entire lines, stanzas, and even poems.

In fact there was only one short period in his career when he was not assuming postures of one kind or another but concentrating his efforts on writing a number of his most important poems and carefully revising others. This period was from 1856 to 1865. From 1856 to late 1859 or early 1860, he composed the new poems for the third (1860) edition and from 1861 to 1865 the poems for *Drum-Taps,* which reflected his response to the Civil War. During the war years, Whitman had served as a volunteer hospital aide in Washington. In such poems as "Cavalry Crossing a Ford," "The Wound-Dresser," "Come Up from the Fields Father," "Vigil Strange I Kept on the Field One Night." "A Sight in Camp in the Daybreak Gray and Dim," and "Year That Trembled and Reel'd Beneath Me," Whitman caught with beautiful simplicity the horror, loneliness, and anguish caused by this national calamity.

The period between 1856 and 1859 is crucial to understanding a significant phase of Whitman's career. During this time he underwent an emotional crisis whose exact details have not been uncovered. Apparently it was this crisis that led to his preoccupation with the theme of "manly love," exploring in the poetry written during this period a decided homosexual sensibility. In the third edition, these poems were gathered in a special grouping entitled "Calamus," which takes its name from the phallus-shaped Calamus plant, or sweet flag, found in swampy, remote areas in the eastern part of the United States. Among the most intense of the "Calamus" poems were "I Saw in Louisiana a Live-Oak Growing," "Not Heat Flames Up and Consumes," "When I Heard at the Close of the Day," "O You Whom I Often and Silently Come," and "To a Western Boy." And written shortly after this period, the revealing "Whoever You Are Holding Me Now in Hand" and the seldom-anthologized and excellent "A Glimpse."

In addition to the "Calamus" poems, he also utilized the "Calamus" theme during this time in his extensive revision of the nationalistic poem "Starting from Paumanok," attempting (unsuccessfully) to rework the poem toward a more generalized statement on the democratic brotherhood of man. In this respect he was more successful in generalizing the "Calamus" emotion in a handful of the other poems that rounded out the 1860 "Calamus" section, such as "I Hear It Was Charged against Me," "City of Orgies," and "The Prairie-Grass Dividing," but these poems are hardly on the same level of artistic achievement as the others.

As an afterthought, Whitman added a balancing group of poems on the theme of heterosexual love, which he titled "Children of Adam." Here he explored in depth the theme he had sounded in the earlier editions, the return to a Garden of Eden innocence in sexual matters. In fact, three of the earlier poems, "I Sing the Body Electric," "A Woman Waits for Me," and "Spontaneous Me," were included in this group. Some of the new "Children of Adam" poems were "To the Garden the World," "From Pent-up Aching Rivers," "One Hour to Madness and Joy," and "As Adam Early in the Morning."

The 1856–60 period was one of great productivity for Whitman. In all, 146 new poems appeared in the third edition, with the thirty-two of the earlier editions carried over.[3] In the third edition he began his practice of bringing together under a group heading poems on the same general theme. In addition to the two already mentioned, Whitman formed the nationalistic "Chants Democratic and Native American" section, which featured such poems as "By Blue Ontario's Shore" (the "Chants Democratic" group title was later dropped and the poems distributed) as well as several other groups.

Among the poems of the 1860 edition was one of his masterpieces, "Out of the Cradle Endlessly Rocking." And in several others, such as "As I Ebb'd with the Ocean of Life," "Myself and Mine," the "Calamus" poem "Scented Herbage of My Breast," and "As the Time Draws Nigh," he reacted to his emotional crisis of the late 1850's with a brooding preoccupation with death. This morbidity was quite unlike the earlier joyous pantheistic view of death of the first two editions, in which, as he had expressed it in the 1856 poem "This Compost" and elsewhere, death was regarded as a positive phase in the evolutionary process, as man

[3] The old Whitman standby, a collection of miscellaneous reviews and essays, was issued separately as *Leaves of Grass Imprints* and distributed gratis by Whitman's publisher to promote the third edition. Hard as it is to believe, Whitman opposed issuing the collection, but went along with it probably out of force of habit. He had in fact become quite aware that this self-puffing device was detracting from the poetry itself and wanted *Leaves of Grass* to be judged on its own merits.

He had earlier approached with great seriousness the idea of appending mixed reviews to *Leaves* to spur sales. The results were less than satisfactory. With nothing to lose, he apparently decided to have some fun with this collection. He included an otherwise favorable 1856 notice by a reviewer who had figured out that Whitman had reprinted in the 1855 edition two of his own unsigned reviews. (Somehow he had missed the third.) He compared their prose style with that of the 1855 preface and with some irritation arrived at the obvious conclusion. The reviewer also accused Whitman of engaging in a literary fraud by quoting Emerson on the spine of the second edition when he had endorsed only the first. "Mr. Whitman," he added, "ought to be ashamed of himself." Apparently Whitman wasn't overcome by remorse, since he included in *Imprints* the three reviews and prominently featured Emerson's letter. Like many others, the reviewer turned from "Mr. Whitman as Critic, to Mr. Whitman as Poet, with considerable pleasure." This was the last such promotional venture for *Leaves of Grass*.

passed from one existence to another through the all-pervading force of nature.

In addition to concentrating on the *Drum-Taps* poems during the war years, Whitman was busy revising the bulk of the poems of the 1860 edition in light of his war experiences.[4] These revisions he made in a blue-covered copy of the third edition, the so-called *Blue Book*. This copy fell into the hands of Secretary of the Interior James Harlan when Whitman was a clerk in the Indian Office of the department. Harlan was scandalized by its sexuality and fired Whitman. Through influential friends Whitman was placed the next day in the attorney general's office. He remained there safe from outraged moralists until 1873, when he suffered a paralytic stroke and left government service to take up residence in Camden. During this period he published the fourth (1867) edition of *Leaves of grass; Sequel to Drum-Taps,* containing the masterful Lincoln elegy "When Lilacs Last in the Dooryard Bloom'd"; the fifth (1871–72) edition; and perhaps his best-known prose piece *Democratic Vistas* (1871).

The upshot of the Harlan–Whitman episode was to provide the poet with his final public role, the "Good Gray Poet," which at center stage he played to the end of his life. His good friend, a volatile Irishman named William Douglas O'Connor, published in 1866 *The Good Gray Poet: A Vindication*. There is evidence that Whitman encouraged this book. Though it made a number of sound points on Whitman's contribution to American letters, the book was so adulatory that there emerged from its pages less a poet than a candidate for sainthood. *The Good Gray Poet* marked the beginning of a fiercely partisan, uncritical approach to Whitman and his poetry by his followers (derisively termed "hot little prophets" by one critic) that has persisted until recent times. Others saw him as a bombastic fraud and a poseur. In short, for many years it was Whitman against the philistines, with the poetry being mainly obscured or oversimplified during the battles.

Following the Civil War and the publication of the fourth edition, Whitman became increasingly preoccupied in his poetry with themes relating to the soul, death, and immortality. He was entering the final phase of his career. Within the span of a dozen years, the poet of the body had given way to the poet of the soul, the poet of intense nationalism to the poet of internationalism and the cosmic. Such poems as "Whispers of Heavenly Death," "Darest Thou Now O Soul," "The Last Invocation," and "A Noiseless Patient Spider" (reworked from its earlier "Cala-

[4] Only six new poems were published in the fourth (1867) edition of *Leaves,* only one of which, "The City Dead-House," was of consequence.

mus" theme), with their emphasis on the spiritual, paved the way for "Passage to India" (1871), Whitman's most ambitious poem of the post–Civil War period. In "Passage," he explored the implications to mankind of the three great scientific achievements of the age, the completion of the Union Pacific Railroad, spanning the continental United States; of the Suez Canal, connecting Europe with Asia; and of the Atlantic Cable.[5]

In the same year Whitman published *Democratic Vistas.* In this essay he replied to Thomas Carlyle's attack on American democracy in *Shooting Niagara: and After?* Like Carlyle, Whitman was disenchanted with the pervading corruption in the United States during the period of reconstruction. However, unlike the English philosopher, Whitman firmly believed in the ultimate triumph of the democratic ideal in the United States.

In 1871–76 and 1881, Whitman published the fifth and sixth editions of *Leaves.* The most notable poems of 1871–76 are "The Base of All Metaphysics," "Prayer of Columbus," and "Song of the Redwood-Tree." In 1881 Whitman settled on the final arrangement of the poems in *Leaves.* Thereafter, no further revisions were made. All new poems after 1881 were added as annexes to *Leaves.* The 1881 edition was initially published in Boston. The Harlan business returned to haunt Whitman when the Boston district attorney threatened prosecution unless certain poems were expurgated. Whitman had been through too much of this sort of thing to cave in, and when he refused, publication of the book was dropped. However, a less timid Philadelphia publisher reissued the book without alteration a year later. The final edition of *Leaves of Grass,* published in 1891–92, is the one familiar to readers today.

With its extraordinary variety of expression and consistently high level of achievement, *Leaves of Grass* invites attention strictly on its own merits. Whitman as poet has finally triumphed over Whitman as public personality. It has not been easy.

[5] Whether "Passage to India," despite its significant theme, is successful *as a poem* is something else again, although with few exceptions critical opinion holds that "Passage" is one of Whitman's great achievements. For dissenting views, see my article in October 1973's *PMLA,* "Passage to Less than India: Structure and Meaning in Whitman's 'Passage to India'"; Newton Arvin, *Whitman* (New York: Macmillan, 1938), pp. 225–26; Richard Chase, *Walt Whitman Reconsidered* (New York: Sloan Associates, 1955), pp. 147–49; Roy Harvey Pearce, *The Continuity of American Poetry* (Princeton: Princeton University Press, 1961; rev. 1965), p. 173; Hyatt H. Waggoner, *American Poets from the Puritans to the Present* (Boston: Houghton Mifflin, 1968), pp. 179–80; and Edwin Haviland Miller, *Walt Whitman's Poetry: A Psychological Journey* (Boston: Houghton Mifflin, Riverside Series, 1968), pp. 210–21.

Part I The Long Foreground

Gay Wilson Allen

The Making of a Poet

> *I greet you at the beginning of a great career,*
> *which yet must have had a long foreground some-*
> *where, for such a start.*—*R. W. Emerson to Walt*
> *Whitman*

1

The "long foreground" which Emerson, in complete ignorance
of Whitman's life, suspected "for such a start" as the first *Leaves of
Grass* has been a subject of speculation among scholars and critics
ever since 1855.[1] The poems which *Walter* Whitman contributed
during the 1840s to popular magazines were so conventional, sentimental, and trite that it seems almost a miracle that *Walt* Whitman
could have written the 1855 poems. Many critics have, in fact, declared that it was a miracle,[2] though they usually called it the result
of a "mystical experience"—which, if genuine, is a kind of miracle.
Although mysticism seems to defy the laws of nature and is still a
puzzle to rational minds, the psychological characteristics of a

[1] Whitman's confession of Emerson's influence, see J. T. Trowbridge, *My Own
Story* (Boston, 1903), 360. Studies: J. B. Moore, "The Master of Whitman," *Studies
in Philology,* XXIII, 77–89 (January 1926); Clarence Gohdes, "Whitman and Emerson," *Sewanee Review,* XXXVII, 79–93 (January 1929); Leon Howard, "For a Cri-
tique of Whitman's Transcendentalism," *Modern Language Notes,* XLVII, 79–85
(February 1932).

[2] Nearly every biographer marvels at the almost unbelievable contrast between
Whitman's poems of the 1840s and those in the first edition of *Leaves of Grass* and
tries to find explanations.

"mystical experience" have been objectively described by William James in *Varieties of Religious Experience*.[3] But Whitman himself in all his reminiscences never mentioned having had anything resembling the kind of experience James calls "mystical," which may be described briefly as the conviction that a Divine (or Cosmic) Consciousness[4] had on a certain occasion (sometimes repeatedly) flowed into a person's finite consciousness, leaving aftereffects which in some cases have lasted for the remainder of the person's life. The only "evidence" any critic or biographer has ever found is Whitman's description of the mating of his body and soul, in a kind of sexual embrace, in section 5 of "Song of Myself." . . .

Even though Whitman's earlier writing gave no promise of the great poems in *Leaves of Grass,* there was, nevertheless, a "foreground" of preparation, some knowledge of which may be helpful in understanding the nature and meaning of the *Leaves.* Even in the home of Whitman's uneducated parents there were attitudes and sympathies which gave direction to the development of the poet. First of all, both parents respected religion, though they were not members of any church and the only sermons they listened to were those of their friend Elias Hicks, a schismatic Quaker.[5] His heresy consisted in his doctrine that no restrictions whatever should be placed on an individual's religious convictions. All Quakers believed in an intuitive "inner light," but Hicks expanded this doctrine to the widest religious freedom. He denounced the doctrine that the chief end of man is "to glorify God, and seek and enjoy Him forever." Man's only duty here on earth, Hicks preached, is to enjoy life to the fullest extent, guided only by the "Deity-planted" intuitions of one's own soul.

This Hicksite doctrine, which closely resembled Emerson's later "Self Reliance," became the very foundation of Walt Whitman's own private religion, and he would always have a tender feeling for Quaker customs, such as the Quaker's proud refusal to doff his hat to man or God and his devotion to plain dress and plain speech. Whitman's maternal grandmother, Naomi Williams Van Velsor, was remembered by her grandson as "my grandmother Amy's sweet old face in its Quaker cap. . . ."[6] The Quakers were at least partly responsible for Whitman's belief that all

[3] William James, *Varieties of Religious Experience* (New York and London, 1902), 379–420. (Reprint 1963 by University Books, same pagination.)

[4] *Ibid.,* 396–399.

[5] G. W. Allen, *The Solitary Singer* (New York, 1955), 7–8, 11–12.

[6] Walt Whitman, *Prose Works 1892,* ed. Floyd Stovall, in *Collected Writings of Walt Whitman* (New York University Press, 1964), I, 7.

physical life is dependent upon and sustained by an infinite spiritual realm about which a human being may have intuitive knowledge. It is not surprising that he later found Emerson a great stimulation to his development as a poet, for Whitman was a "transcendentalist" by conviction before he had ever heard of New England Transcendentalism.

In his youth Whitman had, apparently, little affection for his father. Yet his father in his own blind way also contributed to the "radical" political and social attitudes of his son, who would become a poet. Walter Senior was a great admirer of the notorious socialist Frances ("Fanny") Wright, and Walt remembered having accompanied his father to her lectures in Brooklyn and New York City.[7] In old age he could say of this "most maligned, lied-about" woman, "She has always been to me one of the sweetest of sweet memories. . . . I never felt so glowingly toward any other woman."[8]

Walt Whitman never became a socialist, but his sympathy for the working man, his suspicion of wealth, and his contempt for "polite society" were acquired from his father and such heroes and heroines of his father as Fanny Wright. These early-acquired attitudes also influenced him to champion the "free soil" movement, and to work for the Free Soil Party in 1848 when Martin Van Buren ran for the Presidency and Charles Francis Adams for the Vice-Presidency. This was the cause of Whitman's losing the editorship of the Brooklyn *Eagle,* which was controlled by the "Old Hunkers," the conservative old-line Democrats who dominated the party in New York State. Although Whitman never actively worked for abolition, he did write articles and editorials on the inhumanity of slavery, and the second poem in date of composition to be included in *Leaves of Grass* is "A Boston Ballad," a bitter satire on the Boston authorities who arrested the runaway slave Anthony Burns and returned him to his Virginia owner in June 1854.[9]

The poet of "Song of Myself" suffered vicariously the torments of the "hounded slave" (829–39), and in fantasy brought help to the sick and oppressed everywhere. His compassionate temperament Whitman probably inherited from his Dutch mother, but his politics and identification with all unfortunate people were taught him by his fiercely egalitarian father.

[7] See *Solitary Singer,* 22.

[8] *Ibid.,* 30.

[9] For a contemporary account, see Theodore Parker's *Life and Correspondence,* ed. John Weiss (New York, 1964), II, 125 ff.

One of Walter Senior's personal friends was Tom Paine, who lived in Brooklyn, neglected and even hated by the nation he had helped to win its independence from Britain. Paine's *Age of Reason*—Deistic, not atheistic, as the priests claimed—was one of the Whitman family's most prized books. Walt's life-long anticlericalism was no doubt derived partly from this book, as well as from his own father, but there were other sources for it too. One of these was Count Volney's *Ruins; or Meditation on the Revolutions of Empires,* [10] which regarded the priest as one of the tyrants who had enslaved mankind. Volney was a *philosophe* who contributed to the French Revolution. But what Whitman got from his book, which he had read at home, was less the Existentialism of Volney (man's destiny "is not concealed in the bosom of the divinity; it resides in man himself . . .") than an interest in the history of the human race and the religions of different nations, which Volney surveyed. Whitman learned to respect all religions, without accepting any one, and as a poet he seriously cherished the idea of extracting the best of every religion to form a new eclectic religion to be introduced in his poems. In this new religion for a truly democratic society (more of a philosophy than a sect), man would worship the divinity incarnated in himself.

Another book which Whitman read in his youth was Fanny Wright's *A Few Days in Athens.* [11] He read this book so attentively that he later many times echoed, paraphrased, and perhaps unconsciously quoted it in his poems. Miss Wright attempted to popularize the philosophy of Epicurus by a fictional account of debates between the disciples of Epicurean and of Stoic philosophy, with a final oration by Epicurus himself. Again, only part of the doctrine could have appealed to young Whitman, for Epicurus, like Lucretius, taught that religion is "the bane of human happiness, perverter of human virtue. . . . [The] source of every enjoyment is within yourself. Good and evil lie before you. The good is—all which can yield pleasure: the evil—what must bring pain." Religion denies this doctrine. The so-called lower animals "exercise the faculties they possess. . . . Man alone . . . doubts the evidence

[10] *The Ruins; or Meditation on the Revolutions of Empires,* by C. F. Volney (New York, Calvin Blanchard, n.d.—first published in 1793, rev. 1797), 23.

[11] *A Few Days in Athens, Being the Translation of a Greek Manuscript Discovered in Heraculaneum* [fiction], by Frances Wright (New York, Peter Eckler, n.d.—dedicated to Jeremy Bentham in 1822). For Whitman's use of this book, see David Goodale, "Some of Walt Whitman's Borrowings," *American Literature,* X, 202–213 (May 1938).

of his superior senses . . . and turns to poison all the sources of his happiness." This teaching evidently appealed to the poet who longed in "Song of Myself" to "turn and live with the animals . . . so placid and self-contained" (sec. 32).

Yet in spite of Epicurus's blaming man's unhappiness on religion, *A Few Days in Athens* contained suggestions of a Lucretian naturalistic religion—perhaps causing Whitman later to read *De Rerum Natura* and outline it book by book.[12] In *A Few Days,* Metrodorus declares that "everything is eternal," composed of unchangeable atoms that produce all the varieties in the substances constituting "the great material whole, of which we form a part." The atoms may form part of a vegetable today, and an animal tomorrow, which in perishing forms other vegetables and animals. This is the same doctrine the poet of "Song of Myself" voices near the end of the poem: "I bequeath myself to the dirt to grow from the grass I love, / If you want me again look for me under your bootsoles." But Whitman's joyous acceptance of death as part of the natural cycle of life and rebirth was more like Lucretius's attempt through his poem to abolish the fear of death; death is good because it is natural. In the same spirit Whitman would call the grass in "Song of Myself" "the beautiful uncut hair of graves" (101) and declare that "the smallest sprout shows there is really no death" (117).

A Few Days in Athens may have given Whitman only a few hints, or, more likely, confirmed some of his own intellectual predilections, but some of the parallels between this book and Whitman's ideas in his poems are striking enough to clarify certain themes and motifs in the poems. For example: "all existences are equally wonderful. An African lion is in himself nothing more extraordinary than a Grecian horse; although the whole people of Athens will assemble to gaze on the lion, and exclaim, 'How wonderful!' while no man observes the horse."[13] One of the major themes in "Song of Myself" is that every thing that exists is equally wonderful: "And there is no object so soft but it makes a hub for the wheeled universe. . . ." (1269). And underlying this equality of matter, "all theology with fear and duty in its creed should be banished," for "It is love—love alone that can be claimed by Gods or yielded by man."

---

[12] Whitman's holograph outline is in the Library of Congress, Manuscript Division; discussed in *Solitary Singer,* 139–140.

[13] *A Few Days,* 135.

2

Every influence in his home, his reading, and the demands of his insatiable psyche instilled in the youthful Walter Whitman a revulsion against theologies based on fear and duty and impelled him toward a religion whose only creed was love. This is plainly evident in his memory of the Bible. He must have read the Bible with remarkable attention to have been able to allude to it and quote from it so extensively in his writings, especially in his juvenile poetry and prose preceding *Leaves of Grass.* But it was the New Testament and the God of love which made the deeper impression upon him, to judge by the frequency of his allusions to the life and death of Christ rather than to the persons and events of the Old Testament.[14]

One critic has surmised that the role of the poet as healer and consoler in "Song of Myself" was foreshadowed in the juvenile short story "Shirval,"[15] based on the account of Christ's restoring life to the son of the widow of Nain (Luke 7:11–16). Indeed, the creed Whitman enunciated in his 1855 Preface to *Leaves of Grass* is almost straight out of the New Testament, though modified by Paine's Deism and Elias Hick's radical Quakerism:

> This is what you shall do: Love the earth and sun and the animals, despise riches, give alms to every one that asks, stand up for the stupid and crazy, devote your income and labor to others, hate tyrants, argue not concerning God, have patience and indulgence toward the people, take off your hat to nothing known or unknown or to any man or number of men, go freely with powerful uneducated persons and with the young and with the mothers of families, read these leaves in the open air every season of every year of your life, re-examine all you have been told at school or church or in any book, dismiss whatever insults your own soul, and your very flesh shall be a great poem and have the richest fluency not only in words but in the silent lines of its lips and face and between the lashes of your eyes and in every motion and joint of your body.[16]

[14] G. W. Allen, "Biblical Echoes in Whitman's Works," *American Literature,* VI, 302–315 (November 1934).

[15] "Shirval, A Tale of Jerusalem," in *The Half-Breed and Other Stories of Walt Whitman, Now First Collected,* by Thomas Ollive Mabbott (New York, 1927), 79–85.

[16] Preface to 1855 edition reprinted in *Leaves of Grass: Comprehensive Reader's Edition,* ed. Harold W. Blodgett and Sculley Bradley (New York University Press, 1965), 714.

In this same Preface we find: "There will soon be no more priests, their work is done." But the "superior breed . . . of priests of man," Whitman prophesies, will take their place, by which he means the kind of poet he is striving to become. Eventually in *Passage to India* he will call the poet "the true son of God." The poet who attempted to play this lofty role in *Leaves of Grass* never ceased to draw inspiration from the Hebraic and Christian Scriptures which he so thoroughly absorbed in his youth. What the Old Testament meant to him is indicated in *Democratic Vistas:* "Hebrew prophet, with spirituality, as in flashes of lightning, conscience like red-hot iron, plaintive songs and screams of vengeance for tyrannies and enslavement; Christ with bent head, brooding love and peace, like a dove."[17] No book is more conspicuous in Walt Whitman's "long foreground" than the King James Bible.

Whitman compensated for his lack of formal education by reading so voraciously during his youth and early manhood that it would be tedious to survey all the books and authors he read, and unprofitable because many of them throw only feeble or indirect light on his mature writings, though some probably influenced his intellectual development in deep and subtle ways. In his youth, for example, he devoured the romances of Sir Walter Scott and the sketches and novels of Dickens.[18] His journalistic writings before 1850 often reflected his interest in Scott and Dickens, especially the latter, but *Leaves of Grass* scarcely at all. Whitman read Homer, in at least two translations; also the Greek dramas, Shakespeare, Dante, Milton, and of course the Romantic poets of Great Britain.[19] A great favorite, George Sand,[20] may have given him some hints of the kind of wandering poet he dreamed of becoming, but this ambition was fed by so many springs, personal, cultural, and literary, that it seems almost hopeless to search for the "true" source, and all attempts by scholars and critics have failed. Certainly at one period Emerson's "American Scholar" was one of Whitman's "springs of courage,"[21] as one critic has called it. The 1855 Preface to *Leaves of Grass* has

[17] *Democratic Vistas,* reprinted in *Prose Works 1892* (ed. Stovall), II, 406.

[18] Whitman's newspaper editorials showed considerable interest in Dickens, and in 1842 he defended the author of Boz. *Walt Whitman of the New York Aurora: Editor at Twenty-Two,* ed. Joseph Jay Rubin and Charles H. Brown (State College, Pa., 1950), 114–116.

[19] Cf. *Prose Works 1892* (ed. Stovall), I, 521–523; II, 712.

[20] Esther Shephard developed this thesis in *Walt Whitman's Pose* (New York, 1938).

[21] Haniel Long, *Walt Whitman and the Springs of Courage* (Santa Fe, N.M., 1938).

sometimes been regarded as hardly more than Whitman's varia-
tions on Emerson's theme.

Yet even the ideas of "The American Scholar" could and did
reach Whitman from many directions, for in 1837 Emerson's contribution was mainly to put into eloquent language the ideas and
convictions of the majority of literary minds in the United States
in the third decade of the nineteenth century. The doctrine of
nationalism in art and literature was not confined to America, for
it was a basic tenet of the Romantic movement, from Lessing and
the Schlegels in Germany to Madame de Staël in France, to
Wordsworth in England, and their numerous progeny in many
countries. But the upsurge of American pride after the defeat of
Great Britain in the War of 1812 naturally gave a great impetus to
literary nationalism in the United States. As a journalist during
the 1840 decade, when this nationalism was reaching a frenzy of
intensity, Walt Whitman was bombarded from all sides by appeals
for an indigenous and democratic literature, purified of the aristocratic poisons of feudalistic Europe. Although Shakespeare was
Whitman's favorite author, he would never be able to enjoy him
without a guilty conscience,[22] because he wrote in an aristocratic
age.

In the second issue of his 1855 *Leaves of Grass* Whitman
printed a selection from reviews of the book, but at the top of these
he quoted three long paragraphs from Edwin P. Whipple's 1844
review of Rufus Griswold's *Poets and Poetry of America.* The
prominence of this extract makes it almost a "text" for the reprinted reviews of Whitman's book. In fact, one might suppose
that he proposed it as an "epigraph" (to use T. S. Eliot's term) for
Leaves of Grass, as perhaps it had been for the poet in writing the
poems. The three paragraphs are too long to quote entire, but here
is the substance:

> We can hardly conceive, that a reasonable being should look
> with coldness or dislike upon any efforts to establish a national litera-
> ture, of which poetry is such an important element. . . . The life of
> our native land,—the inner spirit which animates its institutions,—
> the new ideas and principles of which it is the representative,—these
> every patriot must wish to behold reflected from the broad mirror of a
> comprehensive and soul-animating literature. The true vitality of a
> nation is not seen in the triumphs of its industry, the extent of its

---

[22] *Prose Works 1892* (ed. Stovall), Shakespeare poisonous to democracy, II, 388;
feudalistic, 475, 490; early love of, 722, 725, 756; essay: "Shakespeare for America,"
674–675.

conquests, or the reach of its empire; but in its intellectual dominion. Posterity passes over statistical tables of trade and population, to search for records of mind and heart. It is of little moment how many millions of men were included at any time under the name of one people, if they have left no intellectual testimonials of their mode and manner of existence. . . . A nation lives only through its literature, and its mental life is immortal. . . .

America abounds in the materials of poetry: Its history, its scenery, the structure of its social life, the thoughts which pervade its political forms, the meaning which underlies its hot contests, are all capable of being exhibited in a poetical aspect. Carlyle, in speaking of the settlement of Plymouth by the Pilgrims, remarked that, if we had the open sense of the Greeks, we should have "found a poem here; one of nature's own poems, such as she writes in broad facts over great continents." If we have a literature, it should be a national literature; no feeble or sonorous echo of Germany or England, but essentially American in its tone and object.

In order that America may take its due rank in the commonwealth of nations, a literature is needed which shall be the exponent of its higher life. . . . Beneath all the shrewdness and selfishness of the American character, there is a smouldering enthusiasm which flames out at the first touch of fire, —sometimes at the hot and hasty words of party, and sometimes at the bidding of great thoughts and unselfish principles. The heart of the nation is easily stirred to its depths; but those who rouse its fiery impulses into action are often men compounded of ignorance and wickedness, and wholly unfit to guide the passions which they are able to excite. There is no country in the world which has nobler ideas embodied in more worthless shapes. All our factions, fanaticisms, reforms, parties, creeds, ridiculous or dangerous though they often appear, are founded on some aspiration or reality which deserves a better form and expression. . . . We want a poetry which shall speak in clear, loud tones to the people; a poetry which shall make us more in love with our native land, by converting its ennobling scenery into the images of lofty thoughts; . . . give new power to the voice of conscience, and new vitality to human affection; soften and elevate passion; guide enthusiasm in a right direction; and speak out in the high language of men to a nation of men.[23]

Except for the "organic principle" (*i.e.,* poems should grow naturally, like lilacs on a bush or melons on the vine), the substance of Whitman's concept of the nature and functions of the American poet is almost all here in Whipple's plea for a national

[23] Quoted from Whitman's extract, but also reprinted by E. P. Whipple from *Boston Miscellany,* February 1843, in *Essays and Reviews* (New York, 1848), I, 73–77.

literature. But Whipple's expression is formal and abstract. Whitman's genius gave the ideas a more imaginative expression, and converted the nationalistic concepts, already hackneyed from decades of repetition, into the language of poetry.

3

One other suspected or possible source of Whitman's "long foreground" has never been satisfactorily investigated, and remains as elusive as his "mystical experience." In fact, it is the mysticism that many readers have thought they found in certain of Whitman's poems which encourages this search for its fountainhead in the ancient literature of India—and to some extent in other Oriental writings. Emerson may have suspected some knowledge of the old Hindu poems somewhere in the "long foreground," for he himself was deeply interested in the literature of India—and would have detected the striking parallels that other readers soon began to point out.

When Thoreau visited Whitman in 1856, he told the poet that he found *Leaves of Grass* "wonderfully like the Orientals," and asked if Whitman had read them (meaning, apparently, the Sanscrit poems), but the answer was: "No: Tell me about them."[24] Whether this answer was deceptive, modest, or candid remains debatable. Many years later Whitman named, along with the great works in world literature, "the ancient Hindoo poems" as "embryonic facts of 'Leaves of Grass.'"[25] The reference is so ambiguous that one scarcely knows how seriously to take it. Most of the early commentators on the Oriental echoes or parallels in the *Leaves* assumed that Whitman had derived the similarities by indirect influences rather than the actual reading of translations. In 1866 Lord Strangford, a distinguished British Orientalist, thought Whitman's verse technique pure Persian, imbued "with not only the spirit, but with the veriest mannerism, and most absolute trick and accent of Persian poetry. . . ."[26]

---

[24] *The Correspondence of Henry David Thoreau,* ed. Walter Harding and Carl Bode (New York, 1958), 445.

[25] "A Backward Glance O'er Travel'd Roads," Preface to *November Boughs,* 1888; *Prose Works 1892* (ed. Stovall), II, 721–722.

[26] Lord Strangford, "Walt Whitman," *The Pall Mall Gazette,* February 16, 1866; reprinted in *A Selection from the Writings of Viscount Strangford* (London, 1869), II, 297 ff.; see also Harold Blodgett, *Walt Whitman in England* (Ithaca, N.Y., 1934), 198.

Two decades later, the French scholar Gabriel Sarrazin wrote: "Walt Whitman, in his confident and lofty piety, is the direct inheritor of the great Oriental mystics, Brahma, Proclus, Abou Saïd."[27] Edward Carpenter, a British poet who imitated Whitman and visited him in 1877, declared in 1906: "In the Vedic scriptures, and, in lineal succession from these, in the Buddhist and Platonist and Christian writings, in the Taoist of China, the Mystics of Egypt, the Sufis of Persia, the root is to be found—and is clearly distinguishable—the very same from which 'Leaves of Grass' has sprung."[28]

Carpenter even compiled a list of parallel passages in *Leaves of Grass* and the Upanishads, *Mahâparinibbâna Suttanta, Bhagavad Gita,* and *Sayings of Lao-tzu.* But he claimed for these parallels no more than that "all down history the same loving universal spirit has looked out, making its voice heard from time to time, harmonizing the diverse eras, enclosing continents, castes, and theologies."[29] More specifically, an Indian is quoted by William Guthrie as saying that Whitman "must have studied *The Bhagavad Gita,* for in *Leaves of Grass* one finds the teachings of Vedanta; the Song of Myself is but an echo of the sayings of Krishna."[30]

The first scholar to examine in detail the Vedanta parallels was Dorothy Frederica Mercer, who completed a doctoral dissertation in 1933 at the University of California on "Leaves of Grass and the Bhagavad Gita: A Comparative Study."[31] She found a basic similarity in the doctrine of the *self:* "Whitman's soul, like the self of the *Bhagavad Gita,* is the unifying energy . . . it is Brahma incarnated in the body; and it is permanent, indestructible, all-pervading, unmanifest." ("Soul" is here used in the sense of the symbolical "I" in "Song of Myself" and other poems.) Dr. Mercer's study was followed by a more systematic investigation at Benares Hindu University in India by V. K. Chari, who in 1956 completed a dissertation on "Whitman and Indian Thought: an Interpretation in the Light of Vedantic Mysticism"—published in the United States in 1964 as *Whitman in the Light of Vedantic Mysticism.* Dr. Chari found that "The subject matter of Whitman's poetry is no other than the nature of experience itself, an intimate and vital

[27] Gabriel Sarrazin, "Walt Whitman," in *La Renaissance de la Poésie Anglaise, 1798–1889* (Paris, 1889); translation in *In Re Walt Whitman,* ed. Literary Executors of Walt Whitman (Philadelphia, 1893), 159–194.

[28] Edward Carpenter, *Days with Walt Whitman* (London, 1906), 94–102.

[29] *Ibid.,* 250.

[30] William A. Guthrie, *Walt Whitman the Camden Sage* (Cincinnati, 1897), 25.

[31] Summarized, G. W. Allen, *Walt Whitman Handbook* (Chicago, 1946), 459–462.

concern with and a close attention to the fact of human conscious-ness."[32] Chari was not interested in whether Whitman had known the Upanishads or not, but in interpreting *Leaves of Grass* in terms of the ancient Indian logic developed by such teachers as Sankara.

These examples of writers who have suggested Oriental works either as sources or as significant parallels for Whitman's poems have been mentioned to show that his "long foreground" has cast a very long shadow, possibly reaching even from India to Long Island. Whether Whitman did read the "ancient Hindoo poems" in translation, or whether the passages proposed as parallels actu-ally are close enough to be significant, is not as important as the fact that repeatedly intelligent readers have been reminded of various Oriental works as they read Whitman.[33]

4

Not all of Whitman's "long foreground" was useful to him—or at least its use conflicted with other purposes and literary motifs which he strove to express in his poems. One of these influences was the "Young America" literary movement of the 1840 decade led by John L. O'Sullivan, editor of the *Democratic Review,* and a group of literary critics who shared his views.[34] During this decade the *Democratic Review* was friendly to Walter Whitman and published a number of his "popular" short stories and poems. Even later, after he had metamorphosed into an almost totally different kind of poet, Whitman still remembered the magazine with gratitude and approval. In 1858, nine years after the decease of the *Democratic Review,* Whitman called it "a monthly magazine of a profounder quality of talent than any since," especially im-portant to "the young men" of the early 1840s.

The beginning of the Young America movement seemed little more than another demand for a national literature, and O'Sullivan is remembered as the coiner of the phrase "manifest destiny" to justify the expansion of the United States to the Pacific Ocean.

---

[32] V. K. Chari, *Whitman in the Light of Vedantic Mysticism* (Lincoln, Neb., 1964), 18.

[33] T. R. Rajasekharaiah, *The Roots of Whitman's Grass* (Rutherford, N.J., 1970), believes he has found internal evidence of extensive borrowing and adaptation (even unacknowledged appropriation) of ideas, phrases, and passages from Indian literature which Whitman read in translation or in English interpretations.

[34] John Stafford, *The Literary Criticism of "Young America," A Study in the Relationship of Politics and Literature, 1837–1850* (Berkeley, Calif., 1952). See *Solitary Singer,* 127–130.

But the critics who joined the Young America movement were interested in more than expansion and the growth of an empire, or in achieving literary independence from Great Britain. They wanted to use literature to help create a more democratic society—an ideal not unlike that of the Russians a century later in using Social Realism to build a Communist society.

The Young Americans were all Jacksonian Democrats, or Locofocos, as Walt Whitman was also at the time; and because they were strongly partisan, they were savagely attacked by the Whigs as subversive to religion, morality, and good manners. Like all the other nationalists, the Young Americans looked for a poet who would achieve a place in world literature as the American Homer.[35] They scorned contemporary American authors not only for being imitative of European authors but especially for not having emancipated themselves from their aristocratic heritage. They called for a "literature for the people," a "poetry for the mass," by which they meant that their ideal poet not only must be able to exalt the dignity of labor and the honor of poverty, "the brotherhood and equality of all men," the evil consequence of "distinctions of rank and wealth," but also must be able to speak directly to the common people, bolster their courage in the continual struggle against privilege, and foster a truly *democratic society*. Among the British poets they praised were Burns, Crabbe, and Wordsworth—poets who had sprung from the people and spoke their language. Emerson they first praised and then criticized for being too aloof from the life and needs of the masses.[36]

This theory led the Young America critics to focus attention on the poet, the creator of the poem, rather than his creation. How could he understand the people and speak to them unless he himself was of humble origin and had lived with common people? Perhaps this part of the Young American theory appealed to Walt Whitman because he was the son of a carpenter and had grown up in an artisan community. Actually, Whitman nowhere in his published writings referred to the Young Americans and he took no part at the time in their campaign, possibly because he was too busy writing his conventional stories and poems—which did, however, appeal to the literary taste of the masses at that time. In this sense he did "speak to the people," but not the social message which these critics were advocating; yet not because he did not agree with them, for in his editorials in the Brooklyn *Eagle* (1846–

[35] *Ibid.,* 67.
[36] *Ibid.,* 118.

48) he shared most of their social attitudes and patriotic ambitions.[37]

After the *Democratic Review* expired in 1849, the clamor of the Young America critics subsided. It is entirely possible that Whitman never realized that he owed any debt to them. But, as we have seen, in his self-written reviews of the first *Leaves of Grass* he advertised himself as "An American bard at last! One of the roughs. . . . A rude child of the people!"[38] And almost the whole of his 1855 Preface was either an adaptation or an expansion of the Young America theory, as in his declaration that "The largeness of nature or the nation were monstrous without a corresponding largeness and generosity of the spirit of the citizen." This would become Whitman's central theory of the function of literature: to aid the growth of moral character. "An individual is as superb as a nation when he has the qualities which make a superb nation."[39] Whitman never deviated from his ambition to exhibit in his poems the archetype-self needed for an ideal democratic society. Of course, to attain this health-giving influence on the masses he must be read by them, and in 1855 he felt so sure of success in this ambition that he closed his Preface with these words: "The proof of a poet is that his country absorbs him as affectionately as he has absorbed it."

Of all Walt Whitman's failures, his bitterest was his inability to meet his own test of his worth as a poet. In the course of time he came to be praised by friendly critics and biographers as the "poet of democracy," but he would never be read by the masses. His own mother and his brothers and sisters did not understand his poems.[40] Nor did few if any of the omnibus drivers, ferryboat pilots, or wounded soldiers in Civil War hospitals, the men whose companionship gave him most pleasure and satisfaction. That he was indeed a poet, even a great one, was first recognized by educated men and women, especially poets, critics, artists—intellectuals. This is the great contradiction between Whitman's literary theory and his actual achievement as a poet.

---

[37] Many of Whitman's editorials in the *Eagle* were collected by Cleveland Rodgers and John Black in *The Gathering of the Forces* (New York, 1920), 2 vols. A study of Whitman's editorials: Thomas Brasher, *Walt Whitman, Editor of the Brooklyn Eagle* (Detroit, 1970).

[38] *In Re,* 13.

[39] *Leaves of Grass: Comprehensive Reader's Edition,* 710.

[40] See testimony of George Whitman, *In Re,* 35.

5

The contradiction between Whitman's theory (and ambition) and his actual achievement in his poems existed even in the preparatory stages of *Leaves of Grass,* as his notebooks clearly reveal. In the first place, from the very beginning in his new role as "a poet of the people" he was not concerned with average, living Americans but with an ideal archetype:

> True noble expanded American Character is raised on a far more lasting and universal basis than that of any of the characters of the "gentlemen" of aristocratic life, or of novels, or under the European or Asian forms of society or government.—It is to be illimitably proud, independent, self-possessed, generous and gentle. It is to accept nothing except what is equally free and eligible to any body else. It is to be poor, rather than rich—but to prefer death sooner than any mean dependence.—Prudence is part of it, because prudence is the right arm of independence.[41]

No doubt, average Americans also thought of themselves not as they were but as they hoped to be, and Whitman in this 1847 notation epitomized their dream. But few could have had the sophistication to see how far such a dream transcended the actuality. That Whitman did is evidenced by a later notebook passage (probably written a year later):

> Our country seems to be threatened with a sort of ossification of the spirit. Amid all the advanced grandeurs of these times beyond any other of which we know—amid the never enough praised spread of common education and common newspapers and books—amid the universal accessibility of riches and personal comforts—the wonderful inventions—the cheap swift travel bringing far nations together—amid all the extreme reforms and benevolent societies—the current that bears us is one broadly and deeply materialistic and infidel. It is the very worst of infidelity because it suspects not itself but proceeds complacently onward and abounds in churches and all the days of its life solves never the simple riddle why it has not a good time.—For I do not believe the people of these days are happy. The public countenance lacks its bloom of love and its freshness of faith.—For want of these, it is cadaverous as a corpse.[42]

---

[41] *Uncollected Poetry and Prose of Walt Whitman,* ed. Emory Holloway (New York, 1921), II, 63.

[42] *Ibid.,* II, 90.

The point emphasized here is that Whitman the former journalist knew his contemporary society in realistic detail, but in
planning to assume the role of poet of his nation he became a
complete idealist, with the consequence that the America of his
poems is a dream-world, though he fervently hoped to turn the
dream into reality. But he approached this transformation not
through social or political programs but through metaphysics,
derived in part from the Transcendentalism of Carlyle and Emerson. A major theme in Whitman's poems, the Lucretian idea that
the body and the soul are one, would be reached only after much
notebook pondering on the nature of the soul and its relation to
the material world. Thus, in the 1847 notebook:

> The soul or spirit transmits itself into all matter—into rocks, and
> can live the life of a rock—into the sea, and can feel itself the sea—
> into the oak, or other tree—into an animal, and feel itself a horse,
> a fish, or bird—into the earth—into the motions of the sun and
> stars. . . .

Then, more clearly Neo-Platonic:

> The effusion or corporation of the soul is always under the beau-
> tiful laws of physiology—I guess the soul itself can never be anything
> but great and pure and immortal; but it makes itself visible only
> through matter—a perfect head, and bowels and bones to match is
> the easy gate through which it comes from its embowered garden,
> and pleasantly appears to the sight of the world.—A twisted skull,
> and blood watery or rotten by ancestry or gluttony, or rum or bad
> disorders,—they are the darkness toward which the plant will not
> grow, although its seed lies waiting for ages.[43]

But Whitman goes beyond Neo-Platonism in his notebook doctrine of "dilation," which gives the poet's soul the power of growth
without limit or material restriction:

> I think the soul will never stop, or attain to any growth beyond
> which it shall not go.—When I walked at night by the sea shore and
> looked up at the countless stars, I asked of my soul whether it would
> be filled and satisfied when it should become god enfolding all these,
> and open to the life and delight and knowledge of everything in them
> or of them; and the answer was plain to me at the breaking water on

[43] *Ibid.,* II, 65.

to attain this "vision" of the external world, a man's inner
ust be in focus. If he eats his bread in the presence of
men and does not divide with them, his soul will "hiss like
snake, and say to him, 'Fool will you stuff your greed and
e?'"⁴⁷

he ignorant man is demented with the madness of owning
—of having by warranty deeds [in] court clerk's records, the
o mortgage, sell, give away or raise money on certain posses-
—But the wisest soul knows that no object can really be owned
e man or woman any more than another.—The orthodox pro-
r says This is mine, I earned or received or paid for it,—and
sitive right of my own I will put a fence around it, and keep it
ively to myself. . . . He cannot share his friend or his wife be-
of them he is no owner, except by their love, and if any one
hat away from him, it is best not to curse, but quickly call the
cart to his door and let physical wife or friend go, the tail with
de.⁴⁸

doctrine could have come either from the New Testament
he Hindu "scripture" poems. Whitman must have been
ith Emerson's recent (1846) treatment of the delusion of
o in "Hamatreya," but Thoreau's *Walden,* with its run-
e on the tyranny of *being owned* by things, would not be
until 1854. Whatever the source of this wisdom concern-
y goods, Whitman would soon begin to neglect his busi-
s and start preparing to live the role of his ideal poet,
ymbolical purification rites, sacrifices, and moral train-
can we not," he wrote in another notebook of this pe-
beings who by the manliness and transparence of their
isarm the entire world, and brings [*sic*] one and all to his
iends and believers!"⁴⁹ Such a person Walt Whitman
But the charisma he was now cultivating was not that
tian saint or an Oriental ascetic. Several sentences later
e paragraph quoted above he wrote:

he first inspiration of real wisdom in our souls lets us know that
f will and wickedness and malignity we thought so unsightly in
ce are by no means what we are told, but something far dif-
and not amiss except to spirits of the feeble and the shorn.—as
ckles and bristly beard of Jupiter to be removed by washes

67.

68.

the sands at my feet: the answer was, N
want to go further still.[44]

Yet "spirit is not greater than ma
material existence:

> When I see where the east is grea
> sound man's part of the child is grea
> part—or where a father is more need
> me—then I guess I shall see how spirit
> the run of poets and the learned alwa
> ballast of many a grand head.—My l
> which lives is a miracle; but of what I
> limitless and delicious wonder I know
> and call one superior and the other inf
> my sight is greater than my eyes.—
> You have been told that mind is gi
> I cannot understand the mystery.
> myself as two—as my soul [conscience
> same with all men and women.[45]

That "life is a miracle" will be th
sage in his major poem "Song of Myse
he makes his readers *see* by opening t
(their eyes), to the beauties of the ph

> I will not be a great philosophe
> build it with iron pillars, and gather
> make them my disciples, that new sup
> come.—But I will take each man and
> and open the shutters and the sash,
> round the waist, and my right shall po
> ningless road along whose sides are o
> ing philosophy, and oval gates that p
> landscapes clumped with sassafras,
> and every breath through your mouth
> elastic air, which is love.—Not I—n
> you.—It is not far, it is within the stre
> shall find it every where over the oce
> once have the vision to behold it.[46]

[44] *Ibid.,* II, 66.
[45] *Ibid.*
[46] *Ibid.*

and razors, under the judgment of genteel squirts, but in the sight of the great master, proportionate and essential and sublime.[50]

He would be a freckled, bearded Jupiter, not a St. Francis. And Whitman's beard and informal dress would become symbols of his godlike pride in his independence. His confidence in the development of his own soul and body rested in cosmic "Amelioration . . . the blood that runs through the body of the universe." In dramatizing what Amelioration seems to say, he finds his own poetic voice:

> I do not lag—I do not hasten—I bide my hour over billions of billions of years—I exist in the void that takes uncounted time and coheres to a nebula, and in further time cohering to an orb, marches gladly round, a beautiful tangible creature, in his place in the procession of God, where new comers have been falling in[to] the ranks for ever, and will be so always—I could not be balked no how, not if all the worlds and living beings were this minute reduced back into the impalpable film of chaos—I should surely bring up again where we now stand and go on as much further and thence on and on—My right hand is time, and my left hand is space—both are ample—a few quintillions of cycles, a few sextillions of cubic leagues, are not of importance to me—what I shall attain to I can never tell, for there is something that underlies me, of whom I am a part and instrument.[51]

Now he knows that "All truths lie waiting in all things," and that they will unfold to him "like roses from living buds" if he is prepared to receive the truth: "But it must be in yourself.—It shall come from your soul.—It shall be love." The ultimate truth, the leitmotif of his future poems, Whitman has found:

> We know that sympathy or love is the law over all laws, because in nothing else but love is the soul conscious of pure happiness, which appears to be the ultimate place, and point of all things.[52]

6

T.S. Eliot said that mediocre poets borrow, genuine poets steal; by which he meant, evidently, that the real poet transforms what he borrows until he makes it his own. Whitman once declared: "Na-

---

[50] *Ibid.*
[51] *Ibid.,* 79–80.
[52] *Ibid.,* 81.

ture may have given the hint to the author of 'Leaves of Grass,' but there exists no book or fragment of a book which can have given the hint to them [*sic*]."[53] Perhaps he intended only to defend his originality, at a time when too may critics were asking about his debt to Emerson. But *no hint* is too strong a defense, for every author derives hints from many sources, some of which are half buried in his subconscious. However, sources for a literary work are important not because they indicate indebtedness but because they help the reader or critic to understand the kind of ideas or experiences which appealed to the author and found expression in his creations. They may, in short, remove some of the ambiguity of the language and clarify or intensify the meaning which a reader may encounter in it. Literary sources show as much about a poet's character and personality as his manner of composing his poems. Every author reads many books which he quickly forgets because they do not solve any personal problems for him, or they may have only given him confidence in ideas that he had before held with doubt or vagueness. The healthy mind retains what it needs. Sometimes a book can actually change the direction of one's life, but more often it merely strenthens one's intuition and predilections.

The psychoanalytic critic is usually more interested in the author's infantile relations with his parents than in the books he reads a few years later. Both are important, and the books the child reads may throw light on his relations with his parents—and the kind of parents they are. It is significant that in the Whitman home there were copies of *The Age of Reason, A Few Days in Athens,* and Volney's *Ruins.* And, equally important, that little Walter read these books, for there is no evidence that his brothers or sisters did—or if they did read them, the reading bore no visible results.

It is even, in fact, significant that Whitman was an avid reader in his youth. Since he was not ambitious for financial or professional success, he read because he was lonely, curious, or emotionally starved. The second child in a family of six boys and two girls, he may in childhood, as Edwin H. Miller argues, have felt neglected by his harassed mother.[54] By his own admission, he did not feel sympathy for his father until the last years of his father's life (he died in 1855). At the age of twelve the boy left his (probably

[53] *In Re,* 16.
[54] Edwin H. Miller, *Walt Whitman's Poetry:* A *Psychological Journey* (Boston and New York, 1969), 37, *passim.*

uncongenial) home and began boarding with the printer to whom his father had apprenticed him. For many years thereafter he did not have a home of his own, and as Jean Catel has said,[55] the streets of Brooklyn and New York became his home. He found excitement in the crowds and the noise of the city traffic, yet in his teens when he went to the theater he liked to go alone because boys of his own age did not pay close attention to the voices on the stage. Even in a crowd, he lived much in his own thoughts.

Whitman's juvenile writings came, he said himself, from the surface of his mind.[56] He imitated the popular writers of the day and only partially represented himself in the melancholy of his "graveyard" poetry and his didactic stories of insensitive fathers, cruel schoolmasters, young men who succumbed to the temptations of the wicked city, and similar threadbare themes. He did not begin to discover his own literary ability until he began to tap the resources of his fantasy life: his concealed desire for heroic leadership, his need for a symbolical outlet for his dammed-up erotic impulses, the appeal of vicarious dreams of friendship — especially with young men — as a substitute for the intimate friend he could not find in reality, and above all else his yearning for the oceans of love which he felt himself so capable of sharing with someone, anyone, everyone. Many years later (1876), after he had suffered a stroke, partial paralysis, and many defeats in his literary ambitions, Whitman made a "full confession" which explains more frankly than any other confession he ever published the private source of his poems:

> Something more may be added — for, while I am about it, I would make a full confession. I also sent out *Leaves of Grass* to arouse and set flowing in men's and women's hearts, young and old, (my present and future readers,) endless streams of living, pulsating love and friendship, directly from them to myself, now and ever. To this terrible, irrepressible yearning, (surely more or less down underneath in most human souls,) this never-satisfied appetite for sympathy, and this boundless offering of sympathy — this universal democratic comradeship — this old, eternal, yet ever-new interchange of adhesiveness, so fitly emblematic of America — I have given in this book, undisguisedly, declaredly, the openest expression.[57]

[55] Jean Catel, *Walt Whitman: La Naissance du poète* (Paris, 1929), 38–39.
[56] Remark to Horace Traubel, in one of the volumes of *With Walt Whitman in Camden* — exact page not located.
[57] *Leaves of Grass: Comprehensive Reader's Edition*, 751.

This "terrible, irrepressible yearning" was undoubtedly sexual in origin. It may have been stronger in Whitman than in some of his contemporaries, yet "surely more or less down underneath in most human souls." In his preparatory notebooks there is very little about sex, though the basis of the "sex program" in his poems could logically have developed from his Lucretian doctrine of the equality of mind and body, with special emphasis on the sacredness of the body and all its natural functions. But an abstract idea would not have suggested such words as *terrible, irrepressible, never-satisfied appetite* to describe his emotional needs for love and sympathy. One can hardly doubt that Whitman's passional urges caused him to embrace the idea that sex was a healthy, proper, and much-needed subject for a dynamic poetry. Throughout his lifetime many of his readers thought he defied society's rigid censorship of sex because he was depraved. Some early twentieth-century critics thought his defiance a sign of abnormality—and he was aberrant to the extent of exalting "adhesiveness" (a phrenological term[58] for affection between men) over "amativeness" (heterosexual attraction). But in his struggle to understand and come to terms with his own eroticism, abnormal or not, he found out the importance of sex in human experience and had the courage to express his knowledge in the face of enormous social pressure to conceal it.

What Whitman's discovery and his courage to express it meant to literature, Professor Edwin Miller has eloquently stated in his recent book, *Walt Whitman's Poetry: A Psychological Journey:*

> One of Whitman's most original contributions to our (and world) literature is his depiction of the narcissistic universe of the child and adolescent, not in the irrelevant terms of angelic youth with or without "intimations of immortality," but in terms of the dynamics of relationships (or their absence) and sexual maturation. When Whitman insists that the soul cannot be separated from the body he is alleging that man is fated to live by and with his body with all its insistent and frequently contradictory and anxiety-producing desires—as well as with its sensuous delights. . . . When he writes in "Song of Myself":

> Divine am I inside and out, and I make holy whatever
>   I touch or am touched from;

[58] Edward Hungerford, "Walt Whitman and His Chart of Bumps," *American Literature,* II, 350–384 (January 1931).

> The scent of these arm-pits is aroma finer than prayer,
> This head is more than churches or bibles or creeds,

he is protesting the human and emotional damage that results from a culturally imposed rejection of tactility and infantile sensuousness. Casting aside, more successfully than any other American writer of the century, the dark dress of American puritanism and Western inhibitions, he "undrapes" and dances like a Dionysian, or one of the "monsters" in Hawthorne's curiously ambivalent tale of "The Maypole of Merry Mount," to the very brink of Henry James's "abyss," and finds it good because it is human. . . . Whitman . . . rises above the half-truths that afflicted the brooding minds of his [literary] contemporaries: he perceives not only the "inferno" but also the "paradiso" granted to those not afraid of "the dazzle of the light and of every moment of your life."[59]

The "foreground" that Emerson suspected in Whitman's background could not have been this insight into human nature, because he, for all his greater knowledge of literature and philosophy, was one of the most inhibited poets of his period. Only Whitman could undrape and dance like a Dionysian.

[59] Edwin H. Miller, 71–72.

Part II The Creative Process:
Literary Techniques and Achievement

Gay Wilson Allen

Mutations in Whitman's Art

In his provocative Introduction to the first popular reprint of
Walt Whitman's first edition of *Leaves of Grass* (Viking Press,
1959), Malcolm Cowley not only claims that in this edition we have
"Whitman at his best," but he also calls the first version of "Song
of Myself" "perhaps his one completely realized work." That it is
"one of the great poems of modern times" I heartily agree, but I
am also convinced that a few other poems, of later composition,
are also "completely realized."

The problem which this interpretation points up is the
difference between Whitman's poems of various periods.[1] In
addition to "Song of Myself," Cowley admires to a lesser extent
the first published version of "The Sleepers," which he calls the
"fantasia of the unconscious," as well as "To Think of Time,"
"I Sing the Body Electric," and "There Was a Child Went Forth."
Whether these are *better* than "Crossing Brooklyn Ferry," "Out of
the Cradle Endlessly Rocking," "When Lilacs Last in the Dooryard Bloom'd," "Passage to India," and several other major poems
of the later editions is a question that can never be answered to
everyone's satisfaction. But they are more radically different in
content and technique than is generally recognized, and they
should be judged in terms of these differences, which have never
been adequately defined. This essay is intended as a beginning of
such definition, and needs to be greatly extended.

---

[1] I have discussed some of these differences in *The Solitary Singer* (New York,
1955), but nowhere as a specific subject.

Cowley is not the first to regret that Whitman continued until near the end of his life to tinker with his poems,[2] perennially changing titles, grouping and regrouping them, and rewriting and remotivating phrases, segments, even whole poems. Most critics will have to agree, too, that in the first edition we have Whitman at his freshest in vision and boldest in language, "Whitman transformed by a new experience, so that he wanders among familiar objects and finds that each of them has become a miracle." Without disputing the contention that "Song of Myself" is the product of a mystical experience (or experiences), one can say that it details in concrete imagery the objects and sensations experienced by an ecstatic observer of the physical world. It is this very concreteness, even in the long "catalogues," that makes the poem still seem so fresh and "modern."

It is almost impossible for the twentieth-century reader to understand the moral and aesthetic revulsion experienced by most of Whitman's contemporary readers when they first encountered his undraped metaphors: "loveroot, silkthread, crotch and vine," for his private anatomy, and his insistence that "Copulation is no more rank to me than death is." A poet who "doted" on himself, "hankering, gross, mystical, nude," and "belched" his words out over "the roofs of the world," seemed to one contemporary reviewer[3] to know no more about poetry than a hog does about metaphysics. But today, having read many franker practitioners, most readers find nothing to shock them in such language, whether they like it or not. This sophistication, however, makes it necessary for the modern critic of Whitman to insist upon the marvelous accuracy and strength of his imagery in order that it may not be taken too casually for granted.

In none of his later poems does Whitman so acutely convey the felt experience. To take a very simple example from "Song of Myself":

> The big doors of the country-barn stand open and ready,
> The dried grass of the harvest-time loads the slow-drawn
>   wagon,
> The clear light plays on the brown gray and green intertinged,
> The armfuls are packed to the sagging mow:

[2] See Mark Van Doren's "The Poet," in *Walt Whitman: Man, Poet, and Philosopher: Three Lectures . . .* (Washington, 1955).

[3] In London *Critic;* whole review reprinted in *Leaves of Grass Imprints* (Boston, 1860), pp. 43–45.

> I am there . . . .[4] I help . . . . I came stretched atop of the load,
> I felt its soft jolts . . . . one leg reclined on the other,
> I jump from the crossbeams, and seize the clover and timothy,
> And roll head over heels, and tangle my hair full of wisps.

The carpenter's foreplane dressing the plank "whistles its wild ascending lisp." And "The spinning-girl retreats and advances to the hum of the big wheel." The pilot of the ferry-boat "seizes the king-pin, he heaves down with a strong arm." In hundreds of sharply focused images the poet inventories the domestic and national life of the period.

Whitman's almost pathological sympathy also enabled him to convey vicarious experience with remarkable intensity, and was the source of his numerous *metamorphoses*—another link with twentieth-century poetry.[5]

> I am the hounded slave . . . . I wince at the bite of the dogs,
> .   .   .   .
> Agonies are one of my changes of garments;
> I do not ask the wounded person how he feels . . . . I myself
>   become the wounded person,
> My hurt turns livid upon me as I lean on a cane and observe.
> > "Song of Myself"

Whitman's metamorphoses accomplish much more than the conventional, artificial nineteenth-century *personification,* such as the wandering clouds and babbling brooks of Wordsworth and Shelley. In "Song of Myself" the metamorphoses are of two kinds, two levels of association, the one social and the other cosmic, both functioning psychologically. On the social level the poet enters vicariously into the life of every man or woman he has known or can imagine. On the cosmic level he intuits his identity in the evolution of the stars, the origin of life, and the beauty of all elemental things. Thus as he "walks with the tender and growing night" he becomes the sensuous lover of the "Rich apple-blossom earth!" The metaphor is extended with tactile and kinetic imagery. Later, in his cosmical metamorphosis he devours time and space, skirts sierras, covers continents with his palms, and, in a burst of acceleration and dilation, speeds "with tailed meteors . . . . throwing fire-balls like the rest"; finally he departs "as

---

[4] In the 1855 edition Whitman used periods (usually, though not consistently, four) to indicate a rhetorical pause, or caesura.

[5] See Sister M. Bernetta Quinn, *The Metamorphic Tradition in Modern Poetry* (New Brunswick, N.J., 1955).

air," shaking his white locks "at the runaway sun," effusing his
"flesh in eddies" and drifting "it in lacy jags." But the basic metamorphosis is not that of a personality magnified to the dimension
of a comet or planet. It is rather the generative power and fecun-
dity underlying and permeating the universe, symbolized in the
poem by an "I" acutely sensitive to sexual "touch." This was to
remain one of Whitman's favorite themes, but he never found
more successful imagery for it than in this poem, in which the
fecundating orgasm is described as

> Parting tracked by arriving . . . . perpetual payment of the
>   perpetual loan,
> Rich showering rain, and recompense richer afterward.
>
> Sprouts take and accumulate . . . . stand by the curb prolific
>   and vital,
> Landscapes projected masculine full-sized and golden.

The concepts of "Song of Myself" are so large that the critics
have never agreed very closely on what they are, though most
now think the poem is about *the self* rather than *myself*.[6] And
opinions as to the structure and coherence are just as diverse.
But the poet's identifications and metamorphoses obviously
needed both flexibility and expansion in form and language. He
could produce space empathy, for example, only by piling image
on top of image in a seemingly endless procession. Thus the poem
is long, loosely organized, and repetitive. The marvel is that it does
have aesthetic unity and the effect of completion. For many readers it is without doubt Whitman at his best. But the very nature and
quality of "Song of Myself" make it almost inevitable that Whitman can never duplicate the performance. What else can he do
except repeat himself?

Of course he might elaborate some of the minor themes or
motifs in new poems. And that, or something very like it, was what
he did in the other eleven poems of the 1855 edition—or more
accurately, nine, for "Europe . . ." and "A Boston Ballad" predated
"Song of Myself." One of the other poems, "To Think of Time,"
resembles "Song of Myself" only superficially, being concerned
with the pathos of human finitude: "To think that the rivers will
come to flow, and the snow fall, and fruits ripen . . and act upon
others as upon us now . . . . yet not act upon us." Still another,

---

[6] See Malcolm Cowley's Introduction to *Walt Whitman's Leaves of Grass: The
First (1855) Edition* (New York: Viking Press, 1959).

"A Child Went Forth," merely demonstrates somewhat obviously the Wordsworthian doctrine that each of his experiences becomes a part of the child-man, though it has effective imagery. With one or two possible exceptions, the remaining poems of the first edition are not important.

The chief exception is "The Sleepers" (using the later title). It *can* be regarded, in Cowley's words, as a "fantasia of the unconscious," for the dream-imagery drifts, merges, and changes as in hypnagogic vision, and no doubt arose partially, at least, from the poet's secret longings, fears, perhaps even traumas. But closer inspection also reveals an order and structure indicating conscious planning, the kind of planning to be found henceforth in most of Whitman's longer poems. In fact, it is a turning point in his art, a turning to more conscious artistry—sometimes too selfconscious.

Though "The Sleepers" begins as a vision of the sleepers of the world, leveled by slumber and their equality in nature, it becomes an analogy of the transmigratory journey of the soul from its embowered garden of spirit to the physical world and back again to reinvigorating sleep in the womb of time, to await another avatar. "Night" is not so much death itself as the strength-restoring interval between death and birth, analogous to the physiological chemistry of sleep.

> I will duly pass the day O my mother and duly return to you;
> Not you will yield forth the dawn again more surely than you
>   will yield forth me again,
> Not the womb yields the babe in its time more surely than I
>   shall be yielded from you in my time.

Even while Whitman was thus turning to a more deliberate, planned ordering of his symbols and structure, he was misleading his readers and himself by writing prefaces in which he asserted two ambitions that contradicted his practice. The first was a program of nationalism, which led to his playing the role, and finally being accepted as, *the* poet of American democracy. By his choice of imagery he did, as remarked earlier, mirror his experience, his times, and the life of nineteenth-century America. And to this extent he achieved his nationalistic program. But the larger themes of "Song of Myself," "The Sleepers," and indeed most of his poems, are universal: the nature of the *self* in relation to the cosmos and the meaning and purpose of birth and death. These huge themes he could present artistically only by suggesting analogies in nature, which tended, as he developed his art, toward literary designs approaching the structure and function of allegories.

Whitman's second contradictory ambition was to create an anti-art, or no-art; or at least to work by intuition and instinct rather than conscious artistry, which he regarded as artificial, trivial, and false. Like D. H. Lawrence later, he wanted to think with his hips and create with his blood. "All beauty," he said in his 1855 Preface, "comes from beautiful blood and a beautiful brain. If the greatnesses are in conjunction in a man or woman it is enough." At times he seemed to think of the poet as a passive agent of cosmic beauty and truth: "The greatest poet has less a marked style and is more the channel of thoughts and things without increase or diminution, and is the free channel of himself."

But whatever the strength and source of the poet's energy may be, a poem is a *thing:* it has size, shape, and structure. After "Song of Myself" Whitman reduced the size, controlled the shape to a greater extent, and fitted together the parts with painstaking care. His romantic fancy, in the 1855 Preface, that his poems could grow naturally like lilacs on a bush or melons on a vine can be disproved by a glance at almost any of his manuscripts, but this is not necessary to prove that they were shaped by conscious effort and measured judgment. We need only to examine the poems themselves to see and compare their "made" beauties.

The second edition of *Leaves of Grass* (1856) was evidently put together hastily, erratically, and arrogantly—under the double stimulation of Emerson's unexpected praise and in defiance of the public disapproval of the first edition.[7] But it contained one of Whitman's most expert aesthetic creations, first called "Sun-Down Poem" and later "Crossing Brooklyn Ferry." Taking a simple object, such as the ferry, and gradually shaping poetic and metaphysical symbolism out of its physical characteristics was not a new method in Whitman's art, for he had done that with the grass in "Song of Myself." But "Crossing Brooklyn Ferry" has a more balanced symmetry, development, and climax than any poem in the first edition. In one hundred and twenty-two lines he transforms his literary "ferry" into a vehicle for an aesthetic journey from the prosaic shores of Manhattan and Brooklyn to a vision of the eternal destination of the "soul." The physical objects of the East River become "beautiful ministers" to the psyche, each furnishing its part "toward eternity." Some of these "ministers" are the flood tide, the clouds, the sunset, the circling sea-gulls, the

[7] See *The Solitary Singer,* pp. 179ff.

dark patches in the murky water, and the reflections of light on the "scallop-edged waves." To interpret the symbolical meaning of these out of context would make the poem sound mechanical and arbitrary; in context they seem altogether fitting and convincing. This is accomplished partly by letting the symbolical meaning emerge gradually from the natural and literal fact. The poet is describing one of his favorite daily experiences, in which the movement is back and forth across the not-very-wide river separating two cities. But in the poem the forward movement is interrupted by suspension and centrifugal movement, as in the diverging "spokes of light" radiating from the poet's reflection in the water. He merges his identity in the crowd, feels in the "float" sustaining the ferry himself and all humanity dissolved into the flood and ebb-tide of eternity: the endless cycle of birth, death, and rebirth.

> The impalpable sustenance of me from all things at all hours
>   of the day,
> The simple, compact, well-joined scheme—myself disinte-
>   grated, every one disintegrated, yet part of the scheme.

The sense of movement conveyed both by the progression of images and by the imperatives to the river to "flow," "suspend," "expand," etc., carries the sympathetic reader to the completion of a vicarious experience with the poet, the abstract and concrete having operated simultaneously to the speaker's conclusion: "Great or small, you furnish your parts toward the soul."

In form and structure the 1860 "Out of the Cradle Endlessly Rocking" (first published in 1859 as "A Child's Reminiscence") is similar to "Crossing Brooklyn Ferry" and most of the longer poems of 1855, which employ a basic metaphor flowering into an unfolding cluster of symbols. But the great difference is that it includes a narrative, a simple story of two mockingbirds observed by a boy of indefinite age. The poet's retrospective identification with the bird which he supposed to have lost its mate symbolizes his own poetic awakening. To this point, the story is an allegory of the birth of a poet, whose theme is to be unsatisfied love. This is what the poet supposedly learned from the bird, but despite the prominence of the bird in the narrative, it is a secondary symbol in the poem. The primary symbol is the ocean, "the cradle endlessly rocking," the maternal principle, which reconciles the boy-poet to the fact and meaning of death.

This poem is highly emotional, partly because of the pathetic bird-story, and partly because of the lyrical effect of the bird song, which Whitman presents in the form of the aria in Italian opera. No attempt is made to imitate the natural sounds of bird songs, the poet aiming rather at the more subtle effect of the spirit of the song.[8] The language is impassioned, exclamatory, and—a new development in Whitman's art—musical in the strict sense of the term.

> *Two together!*
> *Winds blow south, or winds blow north,*
> *Day come white, or night come black,*
> *Home, or rivers and mountains from home,*
> *Singing all time, minding no time,*
> *While we two keep together.**

This is a new rhythm for Whitman, with its cretics $(- \cup -)$, and choriambs $(- \cup \cup -)$, its tone colors and harmonies, its iterated and balanced sounds.

But Whitman far surpassed the music of this poem in his great elegy, "When Lilacs Last in the Dooryard Bloom'd [1865–66]." Here he used the whole keyboard of his organ, from the fortissimo "O powerful, western, fallen star!" to the pianissimo (the voice of the poet's spirit tallying "the song of the bird"):

> Come, lovely and soothing Death,
> Undulate round the world, serenely arriving, arriving,
> In the day, in the night, to all, to each,
> Sooner or later, delicate Death.

As with "Out of the Cradle," though with greater skill and control, in "Lilacs" Whitman alternates the recitative and aria (speaking and singing lines). In both poems, too, he varies the music and the empathy-producing space imagery by a syntactical device which he perfected after his first two editions. In "Out of the Cradle" this consists of an opening sentence of twenty-two

---

[8] In a very late poem, "To Soar in Freedom and Fulness of Power," Whitman specifically stated the theory on which he created such symbolical music: "I have not so much emulated the birds that musically sing, / I have abandon'd myself to flights, broad circles. . . ."

*Here and in a subsequent reference to "Out of the Cradle Endlessly Rocking," the author quotes from the final 1891–92 version of the poem. The final version contains the opening line "Out of the cradle endlessly rocking," on which the author's main point here depends. In the 1860 version, the line read "Out of the rocked cradle"; Whitman altered it in a later edition.—ED.

verses, in which subject and predicate are held in suspense until the last three verses. The effect of this suspended predication is greatly magnified by an accompanying rhetorical device which he had used as early as "Song of Myself," the reiteration of the first word or phrase of the line (a kind of psychic rhyme[9]), but used more effectively here:

> Out of the cradle endlessly rocking,
> Out of the mocking-bird's throat, the musical shuttle,
> Out of the Ninth-month midnight,
> Over the sterile sands and the fields beyond, . . .

This is rudimentary, however, compared with the use of the same device in "Lilacs," where it is employed with marvelous success to transport the coffin through the lanes and streets, across the broad land, over the breast of the spring landscape. The various motifs—symbolical, emotional, and musical—interweave in a unity transcending variety, all conducting to an inevitable destination, the arrival of the coffin at the grave. The verses continually vary in length, and so do the number of verses in each section, each with its cooperating semantic and musical unit. One example of the symmetry without regularity is the manner in which rhetorical pattern and flowing imagery lead the reader to *feel* the passing of the coffin through the land in Sections 5, 6, and 16, at the end of which the bier comes to rest with a falling cadence.

> There in the fragrant pines, and the cedars dusk and dim.

The "Lilac" poem is a good test of the reader's ability to recognize and appreciate the mutations in Whitman's art. The imagery is less concrete and startling than in "Song of Myself," and natural word-order is sometimes sacrificed for cadence: Whitman would not in the first edition have written "cedars dusk and dim." The lilac has vague "delicate-color'd blossoms" and almost too obviously symbolical "heart-shaped leaves." The bird is merely "gray-brown" and a "wondrous singer." The star is a "western orb sailing the heaven." "Orb" is almost poetic diction. Whitman's diction is now almost as generalized as the language of Longfellow or Tennyson, to whom he had drawn closer in poetic sensibility since writing his 1855 poems. But it is precisely the music—verbal harmonies—in combination with the symbolical imagery, the rhetoric,

[9] See P. Jannacone, *La Poesia di Walt Whitman e L'Evoluzione delle Forme Ritmiche* (Torino, 1898), pp. 65 ff. [Now translated; see Bibliography, p. 151—ED.]

and the modulation of sound that constitutes the originality, power, and aesthetic poise of this poem. The sharp, clear imagery of "Song of Myself" would divert attention from, or even destroy, the mood and tone of this elegy. It is a nineteenth-century master-piece, and the finest composition in his middle style that Whitman ever did, though he later used some of the same techniques in other good poems, such as "Prayer of Columbus," "Song of the Redwood-Tree," and "Passage to India."

The third major development in Whitman's art was the short poem. In the first edition there are no short poems, and no good ones in the second. But in the third (1860) we find many brief poems, some of which are excellent. This edition also gives a clue to the reason for Whitman's turning to the shorter form, and his manuscript notes show plainly the model for his experiments in verse structure.

The best of these shorter poems are found in a group which he calls "Calamus," a somewhat esoteric title derived from the calamus plant, of the Iris family, with lance-shaped leaves, a phal-lic blossom, and pink, aromatic roots that thrive in bogs and marshes. The symbolism is indicated in the first poem of the group:

> In paths untrodden,
> In the growth by margins of pond-waters,
> Escaped from the life that exhibits itself,
> From all standards hitherto published—...
> . . . .
> Strong upon me the life that does not exhibit itself, yet con-
> tains all the rest,
> Resolved to sing no songs to-day but those of manly attach-
> ment, . . .

The symbolism itself is not a new departure, for the calamus plant is only another kind of grass. But the tone, treatment, and poetic structure are a new departure for Whitman. In his manu-scripts he refers to these poems as "sonnets," and when we recall the similarity of the "manly attachment" theme present in most of these poems to Shakespeare's sonnets to his male friend, the con-nection is obvious. Of course an unrhymed poem without definite meter can only resemble a sonnet in its length, concentration, and thematic treatment, and this we do find in the best of these "Calamus" poems, such as the following:

> When I heard at the close of the day how my name had been
> received with plaudits in the capitol, still it was not a
> happy night for me that followed;
> And else, when I caroused, or when my plans were accom-
> plished, still I was not happy;
> But the day when I rose at dawn from the bed of perfect
> health, refreshed, singing, inhaling the ripe breath of
> autumn,
> When I saw the full moon in the west grow pale and disap-
> pear in the morning light,
> When I wandered alone over the beach, and, undressing,
> bathed, laughing with the cool waters, and saw the sun
> rise,
> And when I thought how my dear friend, my lover, was on
> his way coming, O then I was happy;
> O then each breath tasted sweeter—and all that day my food
> nourished me more—And the beautiful day passed well,
> And the next came with equal joy—And with the next, at even-
> ing, came my friend;
> And that night, while all was still, I heard the waters roll
> slowly continually up the shores,
> I heard the hissing rustle of the liquid and sands, as directed
> to me, whispering, to congratulate me,
> For the one I love most lay sleeping by me under the same
> cover in the cool night,
> In the stillness, in the autumn moonbeams, his face was in-
> clined toward me,
> And his arm lay lightly around my breast—And that night
> I was happy.

This poem, however, lacks the tight structure of a real sonnet, and in this characteristic it is a transition to Whitman's mastery of a compact form.

Another group in the 1860 edition, called "Enfans d'Adam" (later "Children of Adam"), was written, as Whitman's manuscripts show, to balance the "friendship for men" group with a cluster on the "amative love of woman." Oddly enough, these do not show the same influence of the traditional sonnet, being either longer and more diffuse or shorter and more epigrammatic, as in No. 14:

> I am he that aches with love;
> Does the earth gravitate? Does not all matter, aching, attract
> all matter?
> So the body of me to all I meet, or that I know.

But in the first poem in this group Whitman achieved a weight of connotation and an originality of symbolical structure that anticipated the Symbolists at the end of the century:

> To the garden, the world, anew ascending,
> Potent mates, daughters, sons, preluding,
> The love, the life of their bodies, meaning and being,
> Curious, here behold my resurrection, after slumber,
> The revolving cycles, in their wide sweep, having brought me
>   again,
> Amorous, mature—all beautiful to me—all wondrous,
> My limbs, and the quivering fire that ever plays through them,
>   for reasons, most wondrous;
> Existing, I peer and penetrate still,
> Content with the present—content with the past,
> By my side, or back of me, Eve following,
> Or in front, and I following her just the same.

Since Charles Davis and I have already given a detailed explication of this poem in the New York University Press edition (New York, 1955) of *Whitman's Poems,* I will merely refer here to a few of its accomplishments in language and structure. Although the poem appears to be more regular than Whitman's earlier poems, the whole approach is oblique—in syntax, rhetoric, and statement. The thought is of the world (human society) returning ("ascending") to the lost innocence of Eden, especially in sexual matters. But this has not happened, nor is it prophesied. The situation evoked is hypothetical—like the poet's metaphorical "resurrection"—and both the syntax and the diction support the implied incompletion.

Many critics have thought the anacoluthon, as illustrated here, the result either of Whitman's ignorance or carelessness, but he used it so many times and so often with effectiveness that we must assume he used it deliberately. Another fine example of such use is in "The Dalliance of the Eagles" (1880). And of course many of the "Drum-Taps" poems violate syntax in order to emphasize the immediacy, the retrospective *presentness* of scene and incident.

The point to be emphasized, however, is that in working on his shorter poems Whitman gave more attention to diction, word order, cadence, and finish. Perhaps his failures are as numerous as in his longer poems, but in "Sparkles from the Wheel," "To a Locomotive in Winter," and "A Noiseless Patient Spider," to mention only a few, he wrote some of his finest lyrics. The "Spider" poem, especially, shows superb mastery. The theme is solitude, and Whitman used the analogy of a spider sitting on a little promontory, surrounded by vacant space, as a parallel to his own human condition. Just as the spider throws out "filament, filament, filament, out of itself" (the repetitions convey the "tireless . . . unreeling"), so does this soul spin its gossamer thread into "measureless oceans of space." But I must quote the whole poem:

> A noiseless patient spider,
> I mark'd, where on a little promontory, it stood isolated;
> Mark'd how, to explore the vacant, vast surrounding,
> It launch'd forth filament, filament, filament, out of itself;
> Ever unreeling them—ever tirelessly speeding them.
>
> And you, O my Soul, where you stand,
> Surrounded, surrounded, in measureless oceans of space,
> Ceaselessly musing, venturing, throwing,—seeking the spheres, to connect them;
> Till the bridge you will need, be form'd—till the ductile anchor hold;
> Till the gossamer thread you fling, catch somewhere, O my Soul.

Notice the difference between "patient noiseless spider" and Whitman's emphatic, deliberately delayed "noiseless patient spider." Throughout the poem the words, the imagery, and the rhythm perfectly fit the spider's action and the poet's almost desperate prayer to "catch somewhere, O my Soul." It is a pleading imperative, not a confident exclamation. "Here," as Mark Van Doren has remarked,[10] "is solitude with a vengeance, in vacancy so vast that any soul at its center, trying to comprehend it, looks terribly minute."

The subject and the symbols remind us of Emily Dickinson, and yet it is such a poem as she never wrote. But to think of the comparison is to realize Whitman's great diversity, for no one would ever think of comparing "Song of Myself" to any example of Emily Dickinson's fragile, subtle art. This poem, no less than "Song of Myself," has space empathy on a vast scale, but the one is painted on a mile-long canvas and the other on the gossamer thread of a spider. The two poems show the vast range in the mutations of Walt Whitman's art.

---

[10] *Introduction to Poetry* (New York, 1951) p. 43.

Roger Asselineau

The Language of Leaves of Grass: *Innovations and Traditions*

Language always loomed large in Walt Whitman's mind. In a way *Leaves of Grass* was a deliberate and systematic attempt at enriching and renewing the traditional vocabulary of poetry. He said so himself:

> I sometimes think the Leaves is only a language experiment—
> that it is an attempt to give the spirit, the body, the man, new
> words, new potentialities of speech—an American, a cosmopolitan
> (the best of America is the best cosmopolitanism) range of self-
> expression. The new world, the new times, the new peoples, the new
> vista, need a tongue according—yes, what is more, will have such a
> tongue—will not be satisfied until it is evolved.

And indeed an analysis of the language which he used in his poems reveals the same mixture of heterogeneous elements of his style. Archaic words are found side by side with neologisms, abstruse terms next to slang words, and foreign words close to Americanisms. Ezra Pound has strongly reproved him for the heteroclite and disparate character of his art, but, in fact, the violence of the poetic flow usually sweeps away the impurities before the reader has had time to notice them or to be surprised by them.

Reprinted by permission of the publishers from Roger Asselineau, The Evolution of Walt Whitman, Vol. II: The Creation of a Book, *Cambridge Mass.: The Belknap Press of Harvard University Press Copyright © 1962 by the President and Fellows of Harvard College. (Original title of this essay: "Language—Innovations and Traditions." Original footnotes omitted.)*

The presence of archaic terms in Whitman's language is a priori unexpected. Is he not the poet of "the Modern Man" for whom the past is nothing but a dead body which one keeps in the doorway for a few hours only before sending it off to the cemetery? If he had been consistent, he ought to have mercilessly rejected all old words. And that is precisely the goal which he set for himself: "I had great trouble in leaving out the stock 'poetical' touches, but succeeded at last," he said of the first version of *Leaves of Grass* in *Specimen Days*. He had made it a rule to "take no illustrations whatever from the ancients or classics, nor from the mythology, nor Egypt, Greece or Rome—nor from the royal and aristocratic institutions and forms of Europe, [to] make no mention or allusion to them whatever. . . ." In practice, however, despite the rigor of his principles, he more than once let pass some obsolete word or in turn borrowed from his predecessors, and the victory which he thought he had won over tradition in 1855 was not as complete as he imagined. Even in the first edition [1855] one already comes across archaisms. Thus he uses "betwixt" instead of "between" and in two places "nigh" instead of "near," "anon," "betimes." He had recourse, too, to words which had long fallen into disuse in everyday language like "to drib," "to buss," "to wrig," "eve" for "evening," and "babe" for "baby." On the whole, however, it must be acknowledged that his language is modern and its character changed very little in 1856 and 1860 despite the introduction of several additional archaisms like "climes," "list" (in the meaning of "to please"), "ere," "diminute" in the second edition [1856], and "loins" and "jocund" in the third one [1860]. In *Drum-Taps* [1865], on the contrary, archaisms suddenly proliferated, as if Whitman had wished to give his war poems the dignity of ancient epics. In particular he used the second person singular for the first time in *Leaves of Grass,* notably in his elegy on Lincoln. He also resorted to a whole new series of archaisms: "kine," "erewhile," "o'er" instead of "over," "to harbinge," "a-gone," "'tis," "cerulean," "lo," with which he sprinkled several poems, and "darkling." Moreover he added here and there in the poems of the first three editions some nigh's and some list's (in the meaning of "to listen") which did not previously appear there. We thus deal with a perfectly conscious refinement. He deliberately renounced the principles of simplicity and modernity which had guided him up to then and now no longer hesitated to fill his poems with borrowed ornaments. In 1871–72, moreover, this process gathered speed. In "Passage to India," "The Mystic Trumpeter," "Thou Mother with Thy Equal Brood" (and a little later in "Prayer of Columbus"), the second person singular abounds. And what is one to make of "Darest Thou Now O Soul" which combines the second person singular with an archaic interrogative form? Henceforth obsolete and "poetic" words become increasingly frequent: "the deep," "e'er," "ne'er," "eld," "haply," "isle," "hark," "to limn," "nay," "'mid," "obeisant," "methinks," "beseems," "emprises," "eterne," "e'en," "atomies," "bale," "charnel," "i'" for "in," "spake," "ope," "longeve," "morn," "benison," "unwrit," "estray," "poesy," "ostent," "brethren," "thereof," and "whereto." In the "Song of the Redwood-Tree" (a specifically American subject though), he even went so far as to evoke the dryads and the hamadryads of the ancient Greeks. But that is not all. He also invoked his Muse, humorously in "Song of the Exposition," but very seriously in "Song of the Universal" and what is even more unexpected, in the poem where he celebrated the locomotive ["To a Locomotive in Winter"]. He came finally in one of his last poems to take for a title "On, on the same ye jocund twain!" in which the last three words belonged to traditional poetic diction.

Thus the vocabulary of *Leaves of Grass* became increasingly conventional. After having wished to innovate boldly, Whitman gradually returned to the tradition. The dignified and high-sounding words which he had at first decided to eliminate from his writings progressively invaded his poems, new ones as well as old. He never discussed this abortive revolution in his critical essays, but apparently, as his inspiration lost its force, he felt more and more the need to fall back on the words which tradition had hallowed and, as it were, charged with poetry in order to enhance the effect of his own verse. Another factor intervened too. . . . His taste gradually became more refined; with age his intransigency and his prejudices lost in intensity and virulence. Though he never completely approved of the works of poets who had remained faithful to orthodoxy like Longfellow, Poe, and Tennyson, he at least became more and more open-minded and even on occasion paid homage to them. The past ceased to appear hateful and despicable to him and, as "Passage to India" shows, he finally came to understand the value of tradition. Thus it is not surprising that instead of trying to break with it he was able simply to prolong it and to re-establish contact with the past by borrowing from his predecessors, from Shakespeare, from Walter Scott, from the Bible, words which, in his youth, he had regarded as dead and dried out. He may also have been influenced by the example of Carlyle, for whom he felt increasing admiration and whose language contains numerous archaisms.

A similar evolution appears in his use of Americanisms and neologisms. At the beginning of his career, he enthusiastically announced: "These States are rapidly supplying themselves with new words, called for by new occasions, new facts, new politics, new combinations.—Far plentier additions will be needed, and, of course, will be supplied." For his part he drew copiously upon this picturesque and savory new vocabulary which permitted him to evoke American flora and fauna and all sorts of customs and institutions peculiar to the United States: "poke-weed," "cottonwood," "pecan-tree," "quahaug," "prairie-dog," "chickadee," "katy-did," "camp-meeting," "Kanuck," "Tuckahoe," "Congressman," "quadroon," and so on. He also wanted to incorporate into his poems the most colloquial words of everyday speech. He recognized no difference between the written and the spoken language. "The Real Dictionary," he said, "will give all words that exist in use, the bad words as well as any." Hence his use of words like "cute," "mighty" (as an adverb), and "duds." But if we class in chronological order, . . . all the Americanisms in *Leaves of Grass,* it becomes apparent that after having abounded in the first two editions, they become rarer in the third and almost completely disappear from the following ones, where a dozen at most can be counted. In this respect, too, Whitman's language became more and more conventional. Not that he ever renounced the principles which he had first applied, but because as his thought became more and more abstract he had less and less need for the richly concrete vocabulary which his compatriots had coined. The evolution of his poetic language tended less in the direction of convention than in that of abstraction. (It is to be noted that in the meantime the language of *Specimen Days* remained, on the contrary, quite concrete and picturesque.) This change, which is manifest even in the choice of his archaisms, which are often evocative in the first three editions, and generally dull and colorless in the others, is thus not merely formal; it reflects the evolution of his philosophy and his gradual passage from materialism to spiritualism.

For the same reason all the technical terms associated with industry and commerce which crowd the *Leaves of Grass* of 1855 and 1856 become increasingly rarer in the poems written after the war, even in the "Song of the Exposition" though its subject was the achievements of modern technology. Besides, it seems that Whitman realized in his old age that he had failed in his attempt to create an industrial and democratic poetry. For he wrote in the preface to *November Boughs* in 1888:

Modern science and democracy seem'd to be throwing out their challenge to poetry [at the time when he began to compose *Leaves of Grass*] to put them in its statements in contradistinction to the songs and myths of the past. As I see it now (perhaps too late,) I have unwittingly taken up that challenge and made an attempt at such statements—which I certainly would not assume to do now, knowing more clearly what it means.

He does not elaborate on this subject and his thought remains obscure. Does he mean by that that poetry should systematically avoid treating these two subject? It is not likely since a few pages later he once more stresses their importance. We should rather conclude then that he regretted at a late date not having been able to better integrate all his scientific, industrial, and political vocabulary in the very texture of his poetry. Too often, indeed, his lists of technical terms constitute a heterogeneous element whose presence in his work seems quite unjustified.

The existence in *Leaves of Grass* of these enumerations and of all the "catalogues," as they are commonly called, poses a problem. . . . They enable Whitman to become conscious of the infinity of space and time and to attain a state of grace, so to speak, but they are also for him a way to indulge in his passion for for words. For at the beginning of his poetic career words exerted an irresistible attraction upon him. He celebrated them in the first edition of *Leaves of Grass:*

Great is language . . . . it is the mightiest of the sciences,
It is the fulness and color and form and diversity of the earth . . . .
and of men and women . . . . and of all qualities and
processes;
It is greater than wealth . . . . it is greater than buildings or
ships or religions or paintings or music.

Yet, for all that, he does not fall into either verbalism or admiration for purely verbal virtuosity. For him words are not mere sounds or signs on the page of a book. As such, he has only contempt for them:

Words! book-words! what are you?

They interest and excite him only insofar as they are the expression and the condensation of an actual experience ("Erlebnis," as the Germans call it so expressively) either directly, or indirectly in imagination:

Latent, in a great user of words, must actually be all passions, crimes, trades, animals, stars, God, sex, the past, might, space, metals, and the like—because these are the words, and he who is not these, plays with a foreign tongue, turning helplessly to dictionaries and authorities. . . .

So each word is for him a fragment hardly detached from cosmic reality yet and still throbbing with life:

The Morning has its words, and the Evening has its words.—How much there is in the word Light! How vast, surrounding, falling, sleepy, noiseless, is the word Night!—It hugs with unfelt yet living arms.

Consequently, it is impossible to replace one word with another, not because each one corresponds to a well-defined intellectual content, but because they all represent concrete realities and separate mystical entities quite distinct from one another:

To me each word out of the——that now compose the English language, has its own meaning, and does not stand for any thing but itself—and there are no two words the same any more than there are two persons the same.

The words of our language are the transcripts of "the substantial words" which are "in the ground and sea," "in the air," and in each of us. They exist first of all in reality and without the presence of this reality the sounds which we articulate are nothing:

I swear I begin to see little or nothing in audible words,
All merges toward the presentation of the unspoken
    meanings of the earth. . . .

Each word is the soul of the thing which it reflects and in that way expresses the spirituality of the world:

All words are spiritual—nothing is more spiritual than words.— Whence are they? along how many thousands and tens of thousands of years have they come? those eluding, fluid, beautiful, fleshless realities, Mother, Father, Water, Earth, Me, This, Soul, Tongue, House, Fire.

There are mysterious correspondences between them and reality. They link us mystically to the world. It is enough to pronounce them to evoke (in the original, magic sense of the word) the object of which they are the symbol and with which we then enter into direct and immediate communication. That is why Whitman calls poets "the Sayers of the Words of the Earth." For his part, he was often content to draw up long lists of them which may appear dry and dull to anyone who forgets what they represent, but which for him were as moving as reality itself. They enabled him to become one with all the things he named in turn and mystically to annex the universe to himself. So they are quite numerous in the first three editions, but after the war, either because he realized their aridity for others, or because they had lost part of their magic power even for himself, he ceased completely to resort to this method of evocation, which shows the decline of his mysticism and his increasingly marked preference for the spiritual side of reality.

Words had not for him only a mystical value; Whitman was also sensitive to their music:

> What beauty there is in words! What a lurking curious charm in the sound of some words!

So he collected them with an indefatigable zeal, noting in particular those which struck him for their picturesque quality or their beauty while he was reading. Thus, coming across "scantlings" in an article, he underlined it and wrote in the margin: "a good word" and immediately composed a short poem in which he played with "scant" and "scantlings." He also carefully recorded all the words which he did not know and checked their meanings afterwards in a dictionary. For instance we find notes of this sort in his papers:

> "euthanasia, an easy death"—"ad captandum, to attract or captivate."

But books and periodicals were not enough for him. He also conducted all sorts of investigations with sailors and workers in order to enrich his vocabulary. The new words which he discovered immediately gave him the desire to compose a poem incorporating them. He formed, for example, the project of writing a whole poem on insects:

> Whole Poem. Poem of Insects.

> Get from Mr. Arkhurst the names of all insects—inter-weave a train of thought suitable—also trains of words.

He was also very much interested in etymologies and discovered with delight the forgotten images from which so many abstract words derive. He never ceased being in raptures over the prodigious richness and beauty of the English language, from the preface to the first edition of *Leaves of Grass* to his essay on "Slang in America" in *November Boughs* in 1888. He even seems to have substantially contributed to *Rambles Among Words* which appeared in 1859 under the name of his friend William Swinton alone.

But a language was a living reality for him, something in constant development which no dictionary could enclose and no list of words exhaust. Hence his interest in slang in which he thought he could catch the language of the future in a nascent state. He fully approved this ceaseless enrichment of the language by the now humorous, now poetic inventions of the popular imagination. Such a process was in keeping with his sense of evolution and his democratic convictions. So he never hesitated to introduce slang words into his poems. He was even the first to use "so long!" in print. New words attracted him irresistibly. Hence all the technical terms with which he crowded some of his catalogues and his frequent use of such adjectives as "magnetic" or "electric." But he was not satisfied with immediately adopting the latest creations; at times he coined new words himself. For instance in 1855 he wrote in the opening poem:

> The blab of the pave . . . . tires of carts and sluff of bootsoles and talk of the promenaders.

in which "pave" is a personal abbreviation of "pavement" and "sluff" a personal onomatopoeia. He sometimes also turns a verb into a noun or conversely, a noun into a verb as the Elizabethans used to do: "the soothe of the waves," "she that had conceived him in her womb and birth'd him." In the first two editions, however, neologisms are still rare (the examples which we have just given almost exhaust the list); they are in general evocative and very felicitously coined because they respect the genius of the language. Such was not the case later. Under the influence of Carlyle, probably, Whitman multiplied them and created horrors, none of which fortunately has survived him: "savantism," "to eclaircise," and "heiress-ship," for instance. After 1865, for the sake of feminism perhaps, he coined a whole series of feminine words in *-ess:* "dispensatress," "all-acceptress," "deliveress," "revoltress," "protectress," "victress," "originatress," "translatress," "tailoress," "oratress." Another of his favorite methods of wordmaking consisted in suppressing suffixes: "apostroph," "philosoph," "literat" (though these last two instances may have been borrowings from the German), "imperturbe" (which corresponds to "imperturbed" or to "imperturbable"), "to promulge." Sometimes, on the contrary, he added a suffix of his own to a standard root as in "deliriate," "oratist," and"venerealee." It was carrying the love of new words a little too far. But, as Mencken has shown, in so doing, he was succumbing to a national rather than to a personal failing.

In 1860 at the same time that he sprinkled his poems with neologisms, Whitman studded them with foreign words, Latin, Spanish, and above all French. We should perhaps see the influence of Carlyle here too, but he may also have wished, in using French words almost always in contexts of democratic inspiration, to indicate his solidarity with the French revolutionists and secretly to link his work to that of George Sand, whom he admired passionately. As for his Spanish words, they were a way of expressing his pan-Americanism. During the Civil War, on the contrary, his preoccupations being exclusively national, he lost the habit of using foreign words, but he returned to that artifice in 1871, at a time when he leaned toward cosmopolitanism — notably in "Proud Music of the Storm," where he introduced a number of Italian words to suggest the music of opera. As he knew none of these languages, he treated them with superb offhandedness, using the word "exposé," for example, as a verb in "I exposé," or creating such philological monsters as "rhythmus," "luminé," "camerado," and "Presidentiad." His friends tried in vain to call his attention to certain errors, but he obstinately stuck to them and perversely refused to admit that he was wrong. William Michael Rossetti in particular once pointed out to him that "Santa Spirita" in "Chanting the Square Deific" was neither Italian nor Latin, but even so Whitman failed to correct his text. Grammatical precision mattered little to him. The sound of these foreign words flattered his ear, which was the only thing that counted.

He also had recourse at times to another source of verbal picturesqueness: words of Indian origin. He seems to have become interested in them between 1856 and 1860. In the notes which Traubel published under the title of *American Primer* and which date back to this period, he wrote:

All aboriginal names sound good. I was asking for something savage and luxuriant, and behold here are the aboriginal names. I see how they are being preserved. They are honest words—they give the true length, breadth, depth. They all fit. Mississippi!—the word winds with chutes—it rolls a stream three thousand miles long. Ohio, Connecticut, Ottawa, Monongahela, all fit. . . . California is sown thick with the names of all the little and big saints. Chase them away and substitute aboriginal names. What is the fitness—What the strange charm of aboriginal names?—Monongahela—it rolls with venison richness upon the Palate. . . .

And he proposed to change the name of Baltimore and from then on to call the St. Lawrence river Niagara. As early as 1860 he, himself, applied this principle in *Leaves of Grass,* renaming Long Island for instance and reviving its Indian name of Pauma-nok, calling New York "Mannahatta." In his old age he still cele-brated the music of this word:

My city's fit and noble name resumed,
Choice aboriginal name, with marvellous beauty, meaning,
A rocky founded island—shores where ever gayly dash
the coming, going, hurrying sea waves.

In the same way he sang the melancholy beauty of "Yonnondio," which means in Iroquois "lament for the aborigines."

Thus the elements of Whitman's vocabulary were numerous and varied. And this explains the exceptional richness of the lan-guage of *Leaves of Grass* which, according to W. H. Trimble, con-sists of 13,447 words, 6,978 of which (that is to say, about half) are used only once. The period of greatest luxuriance undoubtedly were the years 1855–1856 when everything was an object of won-der for Whitman and he tried to put in his work every creation of God and man. In 1856, his book already contained the whole world; so from then on he was obliged to have recourse to neolo-gisms, archaisms, and words of foreign or Indian origin in order to enrich and renew his language. This artificial enrichment, how-ever, did not suffice to make up for the impoverishment of his inspiration and so, for all his efforts at renewal, his vocabulary in fact became increasingly banal and conventional.

Yet, there is one point on which it is possible to discern an improvement: as he grew older, he acquired a finer and finer sense of the propriety of words and of grammatical correctness. In the course of the successive editions of *Leaves of Grass* he cor-rected a number of improprieties which had at first escaped him.

Thus, in 1856, he replaced: "My head evolves on my neck" (where
he confused "to evolve" and "to revolve") by "My head slues
round on my neck." In 1876, he changed in "Song of the Universal": "In spiral roads by long detours . . ." into: "In spiral routes
by long detours . . ." where "routes" is at last the proper word.
And, above all, in 1871, he ceased to mistake "semitic" for "sem-
inal," as he had done since 1856. In 1855 he had treated gram-
mar with sovereign contempt:

> The Real Grammar will be that which declares itself a nucleus
> of the spirit of the laws, with liberty to all to carry out the spirit of
> the laws, even by violating them, if necessary. . . .

In later years, however, he little by little brought himself to eliminate the mistakes which he had made. For example, he cor-
rected as early as 1856 "Was it dreamed whether" into "Was it
doubted that . . ." and while he had at first written in 1860 ". . .
seeking that is yet unfound," he restored the correct form in the
following edition: ". . . seeking what is yet unfound." However,
he waited until 1881 to change "you was" into "you were" in "A
Song for Occupations." Less serious mistakes did not escape him
either. Thus he suppressed "played some," which was a colloquial-
ism, and turned "beside from" into "aside from." He even cor-
rected a construction which he eventually thought too free:
". . . the worst suffering and restless . . ." which in 1860 became:
". . . the worst suffering and most restless. . . ."

Leaves of Grass thus slowly gained in correctness what it lost
in vigor and raciness. Whitman's poetic language followed through
the successive editions of his book a curve parallel to that of his
style and similarly reveals an artist becoming steadily more and
more conscious, more and more conscientious, but whose material unfortunately keeps dwindling with the years.

Stanley K. Coffman, Jr.

"Crossing Brooklyn Ferry": A Note on the Catalogue Technique in Whitman's Poetry

> *The rest is but manipulation (yet that is no small matter).* — Democratic Vistas

Recent Whitman studies have shown so conclusively the existence of formal patterns in his verse that no one is likely now to insist that he wholly abandoned himself to the vagaries of "inspiration" when he composed.[1] At the same time, the characteristics of his verse and his comments on it are so predominantly antiformalist that they persist in discouraging the kind of formal analysis that good poetry requires and thus also discourage the attempt to clarify certain ambiguities in his statement of the theory of organic form. The purpose of this paper is not to deny the drift of his theory and practice toward the antiformalist position, but rather to define more clearly his attitude toward it by studying examples of one of the most distinctive and least carefully analyzed of his patterns or "devices," the catalogue.

[1] Gay Wilson Allen, *American Prosody* (New York, 1935), pp. 217–42; Sculley Bradley, "The Fundamental Metrical Principle in Whitman's Poetry," *American Literature,* X (January, 1939), 437–59; F. O. Matthiessen, *American Renaissance* (New York, 1941), pp. 517–96; Leo Spitzer, "'Explication de texte' Applied to Walt Whitman's Poem 'Out of the Cradle Endlessly Rocking,'" *Journal of English Literary History,* XVI (September, 1949), 229–49. For a complete discussion of various conclusions about Whitman's understanding of formal problems in art, see Gay Allen's summary in *Walt Whitman Handbook* (Chicago, 1946), pp. 375–441, which also includes a "Selected Bibliography" of the work done in this field.

The justification for the "bare lists of words" which mark the Whitman poem is usually found in Emerson's essay on "The Poet": "Bare lists of words are found suggestive to an imaginative and excited mind" (*Essays* [Oxford, 1927], p. 270). According to Emerson, the universe is the externalization of the soul, and its objects symbols, manifestations of the one reality behind them. Words which name objects also carry with them the whole sense of nature and are themselves to be understood as symbols. Thus a list of words (objects) will be effective in giving to the mind, under certain conditions, a heightened sense not only of reality but of the variety and abundance of its manifestations.

It is perfectly possible that a transcendentalist, who sees reality in a special way, might find the catalogue suggestive, though it is worth noting that Emerson qualifies this—an "excited mind." If one is a transcendentalist, he can accept the words in these lists as metonyms; not exclusively or even primarily interested in the form of the poem, he can substitute the sign for the thing signified, or, for purposes of poetry, he can reverse the process and be satisfied with their effectiveness. But not many readers will be content with this; if the catalogues are to be successful, they must function in such a way that their meaning comes from within the poem and not from reference to something outside it.

Emerson's discussion of "metamorphosis" suggests that he was aware of the problem and was unwilling to rest with "bare lists"; but he did not develop the idea of the necessary aesthetic transformation. Whitman turned Emerson's passing comment into a major technique of his verse, but there may also have been some question in his mind about the adequacy of the purely philosophical argument for the catalogue. Occasionally, and on important occasions, he manipulated his lists so carefully that they are not fairly to be described as "catalogues," ordered them so that they became aesthetically expressive, conveyed meaning by their form. The catalogues in "Crossing Brooklyn Ferry" are excellent examples of what he could do with the device.[2]

Two sections of this poem, 3 and 9, consist almost wholly of lists, but they are by no means "bare lists." In section 3 the catalogue begins with the sea-gulls:

> Watched the Twelfth-month sea-gulls, saw
>   them high in the air floating with motion-
>   less wings, oscillating their bodies,

[2] My discussion of the poems is based on the text in *Leaves of Grass,* ed. Emory Holloway (Inclusive Ed.; New York, 1926).

Saw how the glistening yellow lit up parts of
their bodies and left the rest in strong
shadow.

There is an abundance of concrete detail here, mainly appealing
to the sense of sight and the sense of motion. This first image in
the long series begins by directing the imaginative vision upward,
where it is immediately held by the floating, oscillating motion of
the birds, and then is concentrated upon their colors, sharply con-
trasting light and darkness. Out of these details the whole passage
grows. The motion of the gulls continues in their "slow-wheeling
circles" and "gradual edging toward the south"; then is repeated
in the flying vapor, the "swinging motion of the hulls," perhaps in
the "serpentine" pennants, the white "wake," the "whirl" of the
wheels, the "scallop-edged waves," "the ladled cups," the frolicsome "crests." The light imagery, beginning with the "glistening
yellow" of the gulls, extends through the "reflection of the summer
sky in the water," the "beams," the "spokes of light" in the "sunlit
water," the haze and the vapor flying in "fleeces," the "white"
sails, the "pennants," the "white" wake, the "glistening" crests.
"Crests," in fact, contains overtones of *both* light and motion,
as do "shimmering," the "white" wake, and the figure of the "centrifugal spokes of light."[3]

However, the pattern established by recurring images of a
particular motion and a particular color undergoes a change as
the catalogue proceeds, a change effected naturally and realistically within the scene at hand, a sunset scene. The exhilaration
and buoyancy achieved by the clusters of light and motion images
are altered with "The flags of all nations, the falling of them at sunset." The waves are now seen in "twilight," and the imaginative
vision is no longer so markedly directed upward and toward the
horizon; instead, it is necessarily fixed by the failing light upon
what is immediately before it, the docks, the ships in the river,
a "shadowy group." An image pattern carefully prepared for in
the contrast of light *and* dark on the gulls' bodies, in the motion of
birds away toward the south and out of the scene, and in the "vio-
let" tinge of the fleecelike vapor, has now become dominant. As
the sense of motion becomes a falling one, losing its vigor and
soaring quality, so the light, glistening, shimmering, changes to
shadows and darkness and then to the "wild red and yellow" of the

---

[3] The light appears to depend upon the oscillating motion. When the motion
ceases and the imagery conveys the sense of descent, the light becomes fire con-
tending with the darkness.

foundry fires burning into the "night"; the flags fall at sunset, and the firelight, though it burns spasmodically in the night ("flicker" echoes the original, majestic, oscillating light of the gulls), ultimately is cast "down," into the "clefts of streets."[4]

We observe, then, that the images of this catalogue are presented as lists but that the list is not of separate objects, each of which, according to transcendentalist theory, becomes symbolic of the whole. At least, the catalogue does not depend for its expressive value upon any philosophical assumptions about the nature of the word. Instead, the words become effective as they function in the context of other words, which is to say, they become effective aesthetically: they work through a pattern of motion and light, which is first established and then altered. Their status as individual symbols disappears in the sense of a single pattern of motion and light, first evoking exhilaration, which gradually gives way to a feeling of the forbidden and threatening in the fire and darkness. There is no question but that certain of the images are symbolic; the figure of the head, with its halo of divinity, reflected in the water certainly has this meaning; but even this is subordinated to the total effect, which becomes the aim and result of this catalogue.

The changes which take place are more sharply defined when the reader compares this catalogue with the one that concludes the poem. He is struck by the reappearance in section 8 of, first, the "sunset," then the "scallop-edg'd waves," and, finally, the "sea-gulls oscillating their bodies," the "hay-boat" and the "belated lighter." In section 8 these details are only a part of a passage of rhetorical questions, but they (and the rhetorical nature of the questions) prepare for section 9, which is again a listing of details. These, as might now be expected, are basically the same as in section 3. There are the "crested" and frolicsome waves; and once again the "scallop-edg'd" epithet is applied to them, as once again the sea-gulls are seen wheeling "in large circles high in the air." There are the summer sky reflected in the water, the spokes of light about the poet's reflection, the ships, the white sails, the flags; and the foundries once again cast their red and yellow light into the darkness.

---

[4] I have not tried to analyze the sexual imagery to determine its formal relevance to the poem. The importance of this kind of imagery is, of course, obvious, but investigation of it would lead far beyond the limits of this paper. The possibilities for study are, I believe, considerable; note, for example, how skilfully the "cleft" of the streets in "Crossing Brooklyn Ferry," with its connotations of the womb, contrasts with the phallic symbolism of the masts and hills used to invigorate the effect of the second catalogue (after the self of identity has been examined).

But there is also a number of differences. The first is a difference in tone, which derives in part from the imperative mode of
the verb that is used throughout to begin the lines, giving them
conviction and assurance that they did not have before. Though
the objects named are the same, though the sunset occurs and with
it the falling motion and the disappearance of natural light, the
awareness of this is overcome by the force of the imperative—
"Flaunt away, flags . . . be duly lower'd at sunset." Though the
light changes to the glare of foundry chimneys, Whitman defies
this wilderness—"Burn high . . . cast black shadows . . . cast red
and yellow light. . . !" And the final motion is not a falling one; the
fires are commanded to cast their light "over the tops" of the
houses, but not then down into the streets. Other details are re-
introduced in such a way as to reinforce the difference; "Stand up,
tall masts of Mannahatta! stand up, beautiful hills of Brooklyn,"
for example, transforms the masts and hills, previously only mentioned, into images that intensify the quality of soaring and exhilaration in a new and final way.

The two catalogues are, however, so basically similar in imagery that a parallelism between them is inescapable, and they are
further related by the fact that in tone they are the poem's passages of greatest intensity, even though the quality of elation is
lost in one (it does not lose its intensity) and maintained in the
other. Occurring as they do at the middle and end of the poem,
they provide an overall framework, a structural basis upon which
the poem rests. It rises in intensity to section 3, breaks, and rises
again to the climax in section 9, an organization emphasized by
the flat, prosaic statement of the brief section 4, which serves as a
kind of punctuation. And this structure forces the reader to question its meaning. Why is the feeling altered in section 3 and sustained and intensified in section 9? What has happened between
sections 3 and 9 that finally enables the poet to keep his assurance
in the naming of the catalogue's objects? What significance is there
to the inclusion of new images in the final catalogue?

It can be shown that the catalogues not only function as patterns of imagery which have different effects upon the reader as
patterns but, by their differing effects, provide the key to the
meaning of the poem. In other words, they are expressive aesthetically not only in themselves but within the larger overall
structure of the poem. In section 1 Whitman had introduced the
materials of his poem: the flood-tide and the clouds, objects of
nature; the crowds of people, which, like the natural world, are
seen as external to him, to his self. There is no comment other than
this; but he has established the basis for a question that is of re-

curring importance in his verse: What is the relationship of the "I" of the individual identity to that which is external to it? More specifically in the terms of this poem: What is the status of the physical and objective and what attitude shall we assume toward it?

Then in section 2 he dwells at more length upon both external "things" and the "others," considering the human being in this poem, as is clear from his introductory section, from this point of view. Now, however, he *uses* the external, both human and non-human, to heighten his sense of the oneness of all experience, that is, tending to ignore the status of individualization in his concentration upon the unity of the spiritual reality behind it. Uppermost in his mind is the "simple, compact, well-join'd scheme" into which every object, as individual, is disintegrated; in place of things, he sees the "sustenance" derived from them; in place of past and future, the "similitudes" between them; in place of single images, the "glories strung like beads"; in place of the "others," the "ties between me and them." Specifically, he dwells upon the feeling of oneness with the men and women of the future, who will encounter the same externals, the same images; and, since these will be his readers, he is hoping to reach them through the objects as bridges. As usual in his major poems, he is making some comment on the problems of the poet or his poetry.

The direction in which he is moving becomes clear with the opening lines of section 3, which presents the first catalogue, or extensive listing of objects: "It avails not, time nor place—distance avails not." Dissolving the categories of time and space in his contemplation of that outside him, he loses his awareness of its individuality and of his own and approaches the mystic experience of mergence with a transcendent reality. From a short incantatory stanza, continuing the incantatory style of section 2, with its suggestion of a magical invoking of a spiritual reality in which all identity disappears, he moves into the first climax of the poem, the catalogue where the objects flow in upon him, where he becomes them, where a rapport with life is felt through the inescapably positive tone of the passage.

As we have seen, however, the mood passes, is altered; the exhilaration of the opening lines is transformed, with the sense of the original motion falling and failing, in the presence of the foundries, the darkness of the city's streets, as if these were the objects which did not suit the visionary unity and therefore broke the sense of it. There is no question but that the last objects in the list are presented as alien and forbidding, and it would appear that Whitman is now further complicating his subject. In addition to considering the human as well as the natural object, he is to cope with the man-made, the object that is typical of his own modern industrial civilization. After the short series of comments in section 4, whose past tense and matter-of-fact tone admit the change of mood, come the questions that open section 5 and indicate further that his first approach to an understanding of the physical and objective has not been wholly successful:

> What is it then between us?
> What is the count of the scores or hundreds
> of years between us?[5]

The questions are only partially rhetorical. To a certain extent they may be seen as such, suggesting that in the mysticism of the catalogue passage he has transcended time and space (and reached the modern reader). But the organization of the poem, and especially the nature of what follows in its second major division, call for further consideration of their meaning. In section 5 he begins again with the assertion that the categories of time and space do not really matter, but he develops his poem now from a totally different point of view, which in one sense denies what he has just said about them. If in the first division of the poem (secs. 1–3) he has been concerned with an attitude of what in the 1855 "Preface" he calls *sympathy,* he now becomes concerned with its opposite, *pride;* the emphasis now is upon the "I," the self (note, in this connection, his revisions of the poem which cut the "I" from four of the first five lines of the first catalogue).

In section 6, then, he is attending to the self and, with particular reference to the ugly side of identity, the "wolf, the snake, the hog." That this emphasis is productive is clear from the opening line of section 7: "Closer yet I approach you." He is closer to the "others" of the future (as they are to him) for his recognition of the ugly, the sensual, the elements in his own nature normally thought of as separating him from others. And, as these elements are of the senses, of the physical, they create a basis for sympathy for all objects, all "things," as he says: "I too had been struck from the float forever held in solution." This is, of course, a different

[5] In 1881, Whitman dropped from sec. 4 the line, "I project myself a moment to tell you—also I return," which describes perhaps too explicitly what he has just done in the first part of the poem. For the same edition, he dropped a similar line in sec. 3. It is interesting to note revisions of this kind, which show his concern to allow his form to convey his meaning more concretely; compare the decision to eliminate the long passage originally included in sec. 9.

kind of sympathy from that of the first division of the poem, where the physical nature of things or of the self was not recognized as having its own separate and unique character. The metaphor of the float held in solution, which contains the answer to the problems studied in the poem, is crude and difficult to handle, but it is central and deserves special comment.[6]

As the problem of the nature of the physical, objective world is stated here, it resembles the problem of evil, as the transcendentalist might define it, but considered more specifically and realistically than was usual for this philosophy. Whitman recognized very clearly the limitations imposed by the senses, by that which gave his physical nature as well as that of the rest of the external world. The identity provided by the physical gives the sense of life, the awareness of life; but, by virtue of its physicality, it presents at the same time the problem of divisiveness and separateness and the potential for the ugly and evil. Thus evil is regarded in somewhat the same way as in the Christian myth of the Fall, though without placing the burden for the Fall upon man. In order to become man, he must assume the physical, with its limitations; and were he not to become man, the existence in which Whitman so positively believed as the end of all Life would not be possible, the spiritual itself being by itself without meaning or significance.

These implications are more fully developed elsewhere, as in "Out of the Cradle." For the present poem, we find Whitman's meaning expressed in the closing lines, as he addresses the "dumb, beautiful ministers":

> You have waited, you always wait, you dumb,
>   beautiful ministers,
> We receive you with free sense at last, and are
>   insatiate henceforward,
> Not you any more shall be able to foil us, or
>   withhold yourselves from us,
> We use you, and do not cast you aside—we
>   plant you permanently within us,
> We fathom you not—we love you—there is
>   perfection in you also,
> You furnish your parts toward eternity,
> Great or small, you furnish your parts toward
>   the soul.

[6] In his very important study, *Walt Whitman—Poet of Science* (New York, 1953), Joseph Beaver shows the exact scientific meaning Whitman intends for "float" and thus makes certain Whitman's point here, clarifies the connotations which the metaphor had for the poet. The figure remains rather clumsy, I think, perhaps because it draws upon two sciences, but its intended meaning is now clear enough. Cf. also

The conclusion which he reaches in "Crossing Brooklyn Ferry" is that the physical is necessary that we may learn the meaning of spiritual reality but that it must for this reason be allowed to maintain its physical and objective reality; and, though this reality may be seen to have its limitations, these are not only shared by all objects but must be accepted as inevitable accompaniments of the way in which the reality of the spirit can be made manifest. We do not gain in understanding them, *or* spiritual reality, if we attempt to ignore or dissolve their real existence. They must remain objects, dumb but beautiful in their ministering to us.

This would be true of all manifestations, not only those in the world of nature, but those that are man-made; thus the fires of the foundries are no longer seen as alien, or their status as real ignored, but are accepted with all their apparent limitations, like all the objective world. Thus, too, other humans are encouraged to maintain their objectivity, their individuality, in a more balanced, less extremely idealistic view of life. Paradoxically, Whitman approaches the reader of later generations more closely by insisting upon the individuality and objective reality of himself and the reader than by "transcending" this in an idealist's unity. The final catalogue, then, includes the young men, the other humans, and the affirmative images of the city objects, with a clearly defined understanding of their status:

> Expand, being than which none else is per-
> haps more spiritual,
> Keep your places, objects than which none
> else is more lasting.

The overall structure of the poem, on the basis of this interpretation, may be seen to reflect the motion of the ferry, which gives the poem its present title and a background symbol that insures its specific meaning. The poem moves between two extremes, or from one extreme to another, each tested in the presence of the objects of the catalogues. Using Whitman's terminology, the first extreme may be designated as *sympathy,* i.e., loss of the sense of self, transcendence of it, so that the individual soul may become one with the world-soul and experience the conviction of unity in variety. When, however, the objective world is approached in this way alone, it becomes, at the close of the first catalogue, alien; it excludes the poet, who is now, for the moment,

---

Professor Beaver's excellent discussion (pp. 125 ff.) of materialism as a too frequently minimized aspect of Whitman's thought.

separate from it. In spite of Whitman's description of this as the approach through sympathy, it is, for the theme of this poem, clearly not adequate in itself; if it is not supplemented by its opposite, it provides no key to the significance of the external world.

The other extreme is that of *pride,* in Whitman's vocabulary a designation for intense, concentrated awareness of self, even though in this case the awareness is primarily of the unpleasant aspects of individuality. In preparation for his second approach to the external, he assumes an attitude directly opposed to the first one; and, as it emphasizes the physical in him, it leads him to regard the physical in other "objects" and thus to respect their identities as he respects his own (though it is also true that he respects his own more after seeing it as a link between the self and the external world). The result is, as has been indicated, the ability to sustain his ecstasy in their presence and, accepting variety in unity, to identify himself more securely with them, to achieve another sympathy now, which has its source in respect for objectivity and individuality.

As the motion of the boat is from one shore to the other, so the movement of consciousness is, characteristically for Whitman, from an extreme of awareness of soul, which is single and universal, to the other extreme of awareness of the physical, which forms the soul into self and which thus constitutes the basis for the identities of the world. Each of these provides a way of knowing the external and thus leads to a catalogue of objects seen in an ecstasy of understanding. This movement is perhaps to be felt also in the rise and fall of the tide and certainly in the oscillating motion of the imagery in the two catalogues; but it is equally important not to ignore the tone of the closing stanza. Like many of his final passages, this reflects a modification of tone, in that it suggests a more subdued level of calm resolution and assurance, which have been achieved out of the play of opposites or extremes. The poet speaks from a point of view that has achieved a proper balance between these opposites, and thus the poem moves from a sense of unity in variety to the opposed (and for the transcendentalist just as valid) sense of variety in unity, and finally to a steady acceptance of the variety on its own terms. Speaking at the close is the self, the third in Whitman's triadic version of consciousness: soul, body, and a self which is emergent from the interplay between the other two and which can mediate between them as it does here, placing the emphasis where it belongs.[7]

[7] A recent article by Alfred H. Marks, "Whitman's Triadic Imagery," *American Literature,* XXIII (March, 1951), 99–126, shows the triadic nature of Whitman's

The poem, though, not only derives its general sense of balance and organization from the two long lists but also defines its particular emphasis upon the real status of the objective through what happens within them. And what happens within them has little to do with the words as transcendentalist symbols, and much to do with their aesthetic unity, which is the basis for what they say. This aesthetic unity, in turn, sharpens their effectiveness as images; though they are expressive as patterns of imagery changing in one way or another, they have an individual clarity and precision seldom found in Whitman, who, except in certain of the "Drum-Taps" poems, does not often reveal a sharpness of presentation so like what we admire in Thoreau and the Imagists. The care that he took with these catalogues, where he was willing to submit to certain formal requirements, paid off in an exactness of expression that the modern reader too frequently misses in Whitman's poetry.

If the catalogues are not understood, if the reader does not respond to them as Whitman intended, the poem seems not much more than aimless, diffuse, and wandering. Its theme is sufficiently complex that this would be inevitable without careful organization and formal expression. Defining the real and objective status of the external world, and doing so within the framework of transcendental idealism, is a kind of task which requires intellectual effort of a sort that Whitman is too seldom given credit for. But he further takes up the status not only of the object but of those objects which are the products of human society, and of man himself, who for the transcendentalist was a divine but elusive compound of spirit and matter. The close nature of Whitman's thought is not apparent until we recognize this poem as a form of aesthetic rather than philosophic, or simply ecstatic, expression and begin to study it from this point of view. Its form provides the key to its content and, what is more, gives positive evidence that the art-nature analogy, which was the basis for his poetic, was intended to suggest a great deal more than simply the spontaneous and "natural" or even the sense of abundance and variety in poetic composition.

---

universe and its reflection in what may be called a "dialectical technique" that is the basis for his thought and his poems. It is possible to read "Crossing Brooklyn Ferry" in these terms, with the first division (secs. 1–3) as presenting a thesis (sympathy), the second (secs. 4–9) an antithesis (pride), with the synthesis expressed in the closing lines of sec. 9, which allow for an attitude that recognizes the real status of both physical and spiritual.

Edwin Haviland Miller

"There Was a Child Went Forth"

"There Was a Child Went Forth" is one of the most sensitive lyrics in the language and one of the most astute diagnoses of the emergent self. Whitman recaptures the awakening consciousness of the child-poet and the lovely but lonely landscape in which the American child matures. The opening line with its biblical cadence evokes the edenic past and presages the future of the boy who "received with wonder or pity or love or dread." At first he perceives only beautiful natural objects—the lilacs, the grass, the morning glories, the clover. Gradually sounds intrude—"the song of the phœbe-bird" and "the noisy brood of the barnyard." With wonder the child observes the miracle of birth in the barnyard—"the sow's pink-faint litter." Quietly he moves to the "pondside," where he sees "the fish suspending themselves so curiously below there . . and the beautiful curious liquid."

With deceptive understatement Whitman introduces a pivotal symbol in the poem and in his writings. When the boy looks into the water, he is, of course, reenacting the Narcissus myth, like Eve in the Garden of Eden. Unlike Milton, since he is not given to moral judgments or to didactic oversimplifications, Whitman recognizes that love originates in self-love before its evolution into

Walt Whitman's Poetry: A Psychological Journey, *by Edwin Haviland Miller. Houghton Mifflin Company, 1968. Reprinted by permission. Quotations from "There Was a Child Went Forth" are from the 1855 (first) edition of* Leaves of Grass. *To Professor Miller, "the earliest readings* [i.e., *before Whitman invariably revised them for later editions of* Leaves of Grass] *are generally the freshest and freest expression of the original impulse from its unconscious source" (p. viii). (This selection is from Chapter II.)*

outgoing love, and that only negation stems from self-hatred. In other words, he perceives that narcissism with its creative aspects is a complex phenomenon in the growth process. Whitman's "doting" on the self, which has so frequently and simplistically been labeled egocentricity, is better explained in Marcuse's formulation in *Eros and Civilization:*

> The striking paradox that narcissism, usually understood as egotistic withdrawal from reality, here is connected with oneness with the universe, reveals the new depth of the conception: beyond all immature autoeroticism, narcissism denotes a fundamental relatedness to reality which may generate a comprehensive existential order. In other words, narcissism may contain the germ of a different reality principle: the libidinal cathexis of the ego (one's own body) may become the source and reservoir for a new libidinal cathexis of the objective world—transforming this world into a new mode of being.[1]

Somewhat like Proust dipping the madeleine into the teacup, except that Whitman keeps the incident within the framework of a child's limited perception, the boy sees in miniature the totality of his and human life. Unknowingly he journeys to the source, for as he watches the fish in "the beautiful curious liquid" he is observing the fetus in the amniotic fluid, the eternally creative womb of life and art. The fish also introduce the phallic motif, which is invariably present in Whitman's most successful poems: the grass in "Song of Myself," the calamus plant in his love songs, and even the lilacs in "When Lilacs Last in the Dooryard Bloom'd." Here the phallicism leads to the "fatherstuff" in the child's account of his own birth.

In this tightly structured poem, psychologically and artistically, the pond is crucial to the emotional and intellectual development of the child protagonist and to the progression of the poem itself. Similarly, the boy-poet in "Out of the Cradle Endlessly Rocking" discovers the "word," the unifying principle, near the "hissing" sea; and the protagonist in "As I Ebb'd with the Ocean of Life" will have doubts about his identity along the shore. In the "Calamus" poem "In Paths Untrodden," the "I" listens to "tongues aromatic" near the "margins of pond-waters," "away from the clank of the world." In Whitman's verse, then, the pond serves a complex

---

[1] Herbert Marcuse, *Eros and Civilization: A Philosophical Inquiry into Freud* (Boston 1955), p. 169. Reprinted by permission of the Beacon Press; copyright © 1955, 1956 by the Beacon Press.

function, as, coincidentally, it does in *Walden;* and Melville's Pierre writes enigmatically: "Not yet had he dropped his angle into the well of his childhood, to find what fish might be there; for who dreams to find fish in the well?" (Book XXI).

The child in Whitman's poem now wanders blithely in a world filled with animals, "field-sprouts," and "appletrees," when suddenly his idyllic world is shattered. For the first time another human being, significantly an adult, appears, and with his appearance comes fear: "And the old drunkard staggering home from the outhouse of the tavern whence he had lately risen." The drunken motion of the man clashes with the natural order, but at the same time may be the human equivalent of the jerky, darting movements of the fish. Here Whitman's associations are subtle, since the drunkard is linked both with the father who is to be introduced shortly and with the boy himself. The disgusting appearance of the drunkard is to be paralleled in the boy's disgust with his father's craftiness, and both adults evoke fear in the child's heart. The "staggering" parallels the crude description of the father who "had propelled the fatherstuff at night." The drunkard, we are told, "had lately risen" "from the outhouse," and the father from the marital bed. (If Whitman's father was, as some would have it, a drunkard, these associations take on added significance.) But the lonely lot of the besotted man is also that of the child, for as the man makes his uncertain way home alone, so the child sees a group of happy schoolchildren from afar and is not part of the group.

Now the poet turns to the most mysterious and haunting event in his life—his own conception. With fascination and perhaps dread he alludes to "the fatherstuff at night [that] fathered him" and to the mother who "conceived him in her womb and birthed him." Next there is a picture of the mother "with mild words . . . . clean her cap and gown"—one of Whitman's idealized maternal figures. Perhaps the phrase "a wholesome odor falling off her person and clothes as she walks by" is to be contrasted with the somewhat odorous drunkard. From this portrait of the mother we move abruptly to the repellent one of the father, who, as already indicated, embodies the intemperateness and dread associated in the child's mind with the drunkard:

> The father, strong, selfsufficient, manly, mean, angered, unjust,
> The blow, the quick loud word, the tight bargain, the crafty
>   lure. . . .

It matters little whether this passage is autobiographical and literally true, since truth in family relationships is usually the emotional response of the participants. What is important is the self-revelation—the emphasis, perhaps overemphasis, upon the mother's purity and perfection and the ambivalence toward the father, whose genital prowess the boy reluctantly admires but whose "crafty" disposition he scorns.

The section on the family, rightly the longest in the poem, for Whitman is almost invariably correct in his psychological values, is followed by a passage reflecting the uncertainty of the child's "yearning and swelling heart":

> The sense of what is real . . . . the thought if after all it should prove unreal,
> The doubts of daytime and the doubts of nighttime . . . the curious whether and how,
> Whether that which appears so is so . . . . Or is it all flashes and specks?
> Men and women crowding fast in the streets . . if they are not flashes and specks what are they?

Here the doubts and deep-seated fears of the boy are understated, unlike the painful confessions later in the "Calamus" sequence. Just as in life Whitman left home at an early age, presumably because the family provided neither emotional nor intellectual security, so in this poem the child seeks his own answers to his "curious whether and how" when he begins what is to become a familiar journey motif in Whitman's poetry, as he wanders along urban streets and ferries crossing the river. In the course of the journey—and the pattern established in "There Was a Child Went Forth" is characteristic of most of his poems—the child-man in some mysterious way overcomes the paralysis of doubt and arrives at certainty.

Ascending images gradually lead to "light falling on roofs and gables of white or brown," and, finally, to

> The strata of colored clouds . . . . the long bar of maroontint away solitary by itself . . . . the spread of purity it lies motionless in,
> The horizon's edge, the flying seacrow, the fragrance of salt-marsh and shoremud;
> These became part of that child who went forth every day, and who now goes and will always go forth every day. . . .

The reader's eye follows the child-poet in the ascent to cosmic peace and harmony. Here as elsewhere Whitman makes a "leap," as it were, from despair or uncertainty to affirmation. The abrupt transition is perhaps rationally unconvincing, but emotionally there is satisfaction in Whitman's expression of the personal and cultural hunger for an edenic state. Such is the subterranean appeal that we forget that the protagonist finds reality and identity far from the troubling movements of life (the drunkard's "staggering" and coitus), and that, like Melville's Ishmael, the child-man is alone at the beginning and the end of the poem. He, like "the long bar of maroontint" or "the flying seacrow," is "away solitary by itself," a solitary singer in a vast landscape. Thus Whitman creates a lovely rationalization, or sublimation, of human loneliness, which the protagonist (and the poet himself) will endure without a whimper.

To put it another way, the journey comes to its conclusion with a leap that restores the idyllic landscape of the child; the movement, in short, is circular. For the imagery at the conclusion of the poem suggests retreat to the womb. "Purity" and "fragrance" recall the mother's cleanliness and "wholesome odor"; and "the spread of purity it lies motionless in" refers back to the fish in the pond, the fetus in the amniotic fluids. Paradise is regained—through the restoration of the shattered infantile relationship with the mother.

Stephen E. Whicher

Whitman's Awakening to Death: Toward a Biographical Reading of "Out of the Cradle Endlessly Rocking"

> *There is no life in thee, now, except that rocking life imparted by a gently rolling ship; by her, borrowed from the sea; by the sea, from the inscrutable tides of God. But while this sleep, this dream is on ye, move your foot or hand an inch; slip your hold at all; and your identity comes back in horror. Over Descartian vortices you hover. And perhaps, at mid-day, in the fairest weather, with one half-throttled shriek you drop through that transparent air into the summer sea, no more to rise for ever. Heed it well, ye Pantheists!*—Moby-Dick, *"The Masthead"*

I

It is still too little realized that, with the possible but not obvious exception of Melville, no American author has ever engaged in a more daring or eventful voyage of the mind than Whitman. In his later years Whitman himself for some reason attempted to hide its extent, retouched and toned down his most revealing poems and ingeniously fitted them together into a structure toward which he claimed he had been working all the time. This jerry-built monument to the aging Whitman, which remains to this day the

Reprinted by permission of Studies in Romanticism *from 1 (Autumn 1961), 9–28. Copyright © 1962 by the Trustees of Boston University.*

basis of nearly all anthologies of his work and is still reverently toured by uncritical guides, is actually a major obstacle to the recognition of his true stature. Fortunately a strong critical tradition[1] has now for many years been working to lay bare for us the real structure of Whitman's work, the spiritual biography that emerges from a comparative reading of all the editions of his *Leaves.* In this paper I wish to re-examine some part of this story as it emerges from certain key poems of the 1855 and 1860 editions, in particular "Out of the Cradle."[2]

For this purpose it is convenient to accept the periods, or phases, which Floyd Stovall distinguished nearly thirty years ago[3] and which time has only confirmed (the names are mine): Whitman's first or transcendental phase runs from 1855 through 1858; the second or tragic phase begins with 1859 and runs through the first publication of "When Lilacs Last" in 1865; the third or philosophic phase comprises the rest of his poetic career. This is the framework of the discussion that follows, which will center on the years 1855–60. In these years, I shall argue, it is not enough to say that a new note entered Whitman's work or that he passed through a time of serious trouble; the whole character of his work was radically and permanently altered. To trace this change in the

[1] See particularly Jean Catel, *Walt Whitman: La Naissance du Poète* (Paris, 1929); Frederik Schyberg, *Walt Whitman* (Copenhagen, 1933), trans. Evie Allison Allen (New York, 1951); and Roger Asselineau, *L'évolution de Walt Whitman après la première édition des Feuilles d'Herbe* (Paris, 1954), Part I trans. and rev. as *The Evolution of Walt Whitman: The Creation of a Personality* (Cambridge, Mass., 1960) [and Part II as *The Creation of a Book,* 1962]. This paper starts from their essential conclusions and attempts to take a further step. In particular, it accepts without argument Schyberg's conjecture of an emotional crisis between 1857 and 1860 and of some sort of homosexual "love affair" to explain it, and uses this assumption as a basis for the interpretation of some of the poems from which it was first conjectured. For the resulting hypothesis, sometimes for convenience stated as if it were fact, I ask only the minimum privilege of any such construction, a willing suspension of disbelief for long enough to make the statement possible. For convenience also, I write often as if the actual Whitman and the speaker in his poems were one and the same. Though I hope I may be permitted such shorthand devices in this brief paper, a full statement of these matters should of course constantly remind us that we are charting the drift of a highly active imagination, not reconstructing actual events.

[2] A version of this paper was read at the English Institute on September 6, 1960, as the first in a symposium on "Out of the Cradle." [Reprinted in *The Presence of Walt Whitman,* ed. R. W. B. Lewis; see Bibliography, below.]

[3] Floyd Stovall, "Main Drifts in Whitman's Poetry," *American Literature,* IV (1932), 3–21.

space I have I will focus on one theme only, what Asselineau calls Whitman's obsession with death.[4]

A major theme of the poems of the first phase, of course, is the poet's victory over death. In every possible way these poems deny the finality of death and proclaim immortality. In this they make particularly plain what Schyberg has called Whitman's "optimism in defiance,"[5] for a preoccupation with death marks not merely the young Whitman's Emmeline Grangerford period but later apprentice work, too, and is evidenced in the early *Leaves* themselves in the very frequency with which his victory has to be re-enacted. The thought of death was clearly the chief threat his vision had to overcome. It did so not by doctrine nor any merely conceptual means but by lifting him to a Life that in its own nature contradicted death. He was relieved of his fear of death by becoming one with a life-force to which death simply *was not*.

The logic of his position is stated by Emerson, whose service to the reader of Whitman is often to give conceptual definition to attitudes and insights which are too close to Whitman for definition, which he does not state because he lives them. Immortality, for Emerson, has nothing to do with duration or continuance. Rather it is "an intellectual quality," or even "an energy."

> He has it, and he alone, who gives life to all names, persons, things, where he comes. No religion, not the wildest mythology dies for him; no art is lost. He vivifies what he touches. Future state is an illusion for the ever-present state. It is not length of life, but depth of life. It is not duration, but a taking of the soul out of time, as all high action of the mind does: when we are living in the sentiments we ask no questions about time. The spiritual world takes place;—that which is always the same.[6]

Is this not equally the position of Whitman, whom Emerson might as well have been describing in this passage? In those first years Whitman could merge with an energy to which death was an irrelevance.

Of course we must translate a bit. Emerson's concept of a qualitative immortality is essentially ethical, a neo-stoicism, while

[4] *L'évolution,* pp. 344–359; [The Evolution, II, 61–77].

[5] Allen, p. 59. Cf. Gay Wilson Allen, *Walt Whitman Handbook* (Chicago, 1946), p. 124.

[6] "Immortality," *Letters and Social Aims,* in *Complete Works,* Centenary Edition (Boston and New York, 1904), VIII, 347.

Whitman's experience of it is an instinctive release of soul that carries no particular ethical condition except that one be capable of achieving it. One consequence is that the Life Whitman enters encompasses all time but is not out of time altogether, as is Emerson's. Lifted on its flood Whitman acquires a cosmic memory and a godlike prevision and can move backward and forward at will through the remotest ages. Unlike Emerson's Over-Soul, for which history is biography, the biography of Whitman's "Me myself" is history, but it is equally deathless since it is the life-force itself. Essentially, it brings him the same assurance, an ever-present Life beside which death is simply unreal.

Yet the force of this kind of transcendental vision derives partly from the fact that it *is* vision; Whitman holds to it so strongly because he is also aware that in his actual existence he continues to hover over the universal plunge into annihilation. Man's vision can transcend his mortal condition but cannot change it. Emerson confronted this fact and confessed he had nothing very helpful to say about it. "The event of death is always astounding; our philosophy never reaches, never possesses it; we are always at the beginning of our catechism; always the definition is yet to be made."[7] The best he could do was to repeat his ethical talisman, "Think on living." "Simply I have nothing to do" with "that question of another life." Whitman, I would say, takes the same position but because of the existential mode in which he writes can defend it more powerfully, if also more confusingly.

In Emerson's terms, it is the Reason that sees the ever-present immortality while the Understanding can see only the event of death. Both are right, but the poet by a fable can entice the Understanding out of its fears and so, as Plato put it, charm the child in the soul. This is the true function of those suggestions of a future state that certainly are to be found everywhere in these poems. Does Whitman, for example, believe in metempsychosis, as is so often asserted? It is hard to deny it, yet I would suggest that such a statement of the matter misses the point. These hints and guesses are bits of fable, *mythos,* "as-if" fragments scattered on the waters for the Understanding to cling to and support its unbelief. They are preparatory, instrumental, "indirect," intended not to assert anything directly but to throw the mind into the proper attitude to move beyond their metaphoric suggestions into the inwardness of pure truth. When Whitman exclaims of the dead, for example,

[7] *Journals* (Cambridge, Mass., 1910), IV, 343.

"They are alive and well somewhere," his intention is not to tell us some fact but to stir us to feel about the dead *as if* that were the fact. All these hints of belief in the future that are thrown off from the first-phase poems, like sparkles from a pinwheel, are best taken as a measure of Whitman's confidence, exuberant enactments of the power and endless life which is his *now*. Essentially the faith from which they spring is self-sustaining and needs no doctrine to prop it; as Emerson said, the faith is the evidence. Life is; death is not: that is all Whitman knows or needs to know.

Such faith by inspection has the advantage that it is not tied to any formula and is not refutable by any argument. Its disadvantage is that it tends to die with the inspiration that brings it. The visionary gleam comes and goes by laws of its own, and each time it goes it leaves its votary face to face with the same spiritual emergency. It is not simply that the vision dies and is replaced by the unaltered facts it had denied. Vision itself is treacherous. A man may "loafe and invite" his soul but he cannot predict or control what will accept the invitation. Vision may be demonic as well as transcendental, a nightmare confirmation of dread instead of a release of power and hope.

Both modes of vision are strong in Whitman from the beginning of his work; the stronger the poem, the more its dynamics are controlled by the battle between the two. In the 1855 poems the transcendental mode is dominant and the demonic recessive, but its concealed strength is great. It shows its teeth everywhere in "Song of Myself," something like one-fifteenth of the whole being of this character. More significant than its amount is its position. It touches with its threat the key passage on the meaning of the grass; it creeps in intermittently to darken the catalogues; and in the central sections it seizes control of the poem altogether and hammers at the poet with image after image of agony and defeat ("O Christ! My fit is mastering me!") until, cuffed and stunned, he wins a moment's respite and in that interval the transcendental vision sweeps back "replenished with supreme power." Even at the end, though no longer with power to alarm, a breath of nightmare returns and the poet must reconfirm his victory:

> Of the turbid pool that lies in the autumn forest,
> Of the moon that descends the steeps of the soughing twilight,
> Toss, sparkles of day and dusk . . . . toss on the black stems
>   that decay in the muck,
> Toss to the moaning gibberish of the dry limbs.

> I ascend from the moon . . . . I ascend from the night,
> And perceive of the ghastly glitter the sunbeams reflected,
> And debouch to the steady and central from the offspring
>   great or small.[8]

This dark element in the poem is by no means incidental; it is the enemy the hero exists to fight. "Song of Myself" is the epic of his victory. As with all Titanic heroes, as with the angels in *Paradise Lost,* his struggle is a bit unconvincing since we cannot really believe in the possibility of his defeat. But this appearance of invincibility is the true illusion, not the threat to it. That is supported not merely by the worldly trippers and askers around him but by the voices of doubt within him, "saying / That this was all folly." The hero's victory is earned; his power is needed; his air of omnipotence is the euphoria of a danger overcome.

If "Song of Myself" did not in itself tell us this, as it does, another poem of the 1855 edition makes it plain, the great companion piece to "Song of Myself" which Whitman eventually called "The Sleepers." That this poem also, like the other poems of this volume, brings us to the security which they were all written to celebrate should not prevent us from seeing that it does so by a very different road. The first line, "I wander all night in my vision," sounds like the start of a section of "Song of Myself," but we quickly see that this is not the same "I" nor the same vision: "Wandering and confused . . . . lost to myself . . . . ill-assorted . . . . contradictory." This "I" is not "Myself" but is "lost to myself." It is a night consciousness, troubled, confused, disembodied, will-less and disorganized like the mind in sleep. The expansive energy of "Song of Myself" is withdrawn from this poem; the speaker here is passive and powerless. He is therefore *exposed* in a way the hero of "Song of Myself" was not. He encounters at once images of death and defeat:

---

[8] All quotations in this paper are from the earliest published version of the poem cited: the 1855 version of "Song of Myself" and "The Sleepers," the 1860 version of "As I Ebb'd," that or the MS version of "Scented Herbage," and for "Out of the Cradle," the poem entitled "A Child's Reminiscence" which was published in the *Saturday Press* for December 27, 1859, and republished by Thomas O. Mabbott and Rollo G. Silver, University of Washington Quartos, No. I (Seattle, 1930). For clarity, however, I use the final titles. I have tried to read these poems without preconceptions imported from the more familiar revised versions, and I must ask anyone who would examine my conclusions to do the same.

> The wretched features of ennuyees, the white features of
> corpses, the livid faces of drunkards, the sick-gray faces
> of onanists,
> The gashed bodies on battlefields, the insane in their strong-
> doored rooms, the sacred idiots. . . .

Eighteen of the twenty-five classes of sleeper specified in the first twenty-six lines of the poem are disturbing in some way, samples of evil, distress, or death. The center of this poem, we soon see, is not life but death. The chief sleeper is the transcendental assurance of life that controls "Song of Myself." That poem had said, not without a struggle, "The dead are not dead." "The Sleepers" says, "Here they lie." Quite deliberately, I think, Whitman here permits to speak the darker under-consciousness which his waking vision had put down but which remained and must remain part of his truth.

The chief evidence for this conclusion is the long section of the poem, following the introductory description of the sleepers as they lie "stretched and still," in which the poet somnambulistically enters and becomes a succession of dreams. Though the fiction of this section is that these are a miscellaneous sample of the dreams of a number of people, we cannot get very far into it without realizing that they look more like the dreams of one consciousness. Certain points can be made about them: (1) They are connected by numerous ties of detail, action, and mood and can be made with little forcing to tell a continuous story, a story which, as is appropriate to the unconscious autobiography that emerges in such dreams, is essentially an oedipal one. (2) Their dominant mood is one of anxiety and guilt; one after another they present images of disaster and loss. Even when the poet makes a visible effort to extricate himself from their oppression it continues to control him, modulating at last into the murderous anger that is concomitant with such feelings. (3) Certain of the individual dreams seem to offer a deliberate contrast to "Song of Myself." During the sermon that concludes "Song of Myself," for example, the prophet-god says to his disciple,

> Long have you timidly waded, holding a plank by the shore,
> Now I will you to be a bold swimmer,
> To jump off in the midst of the sea, and rise again and nod to
> me and shout, and laughingly dash with your hair.

Now this bold swimmer returns, only to be dashed on the rocks and killed, while the dreamer watches helplessly from the shore. And a few lines earlier, when the dreamer has become a shroud to wrap a body in the grave, the grave does not "multiply what has been confided" to it, nor does the corpse rise.

> It seems to me that everything in the light and air ought to be
>   happy;
> Whoever is not in his coffin and the dark grave, let him know
>   he has enough.

In this part of the poem Whitman does not merely return to the thought of death but reveals through these dreams some of the reasons for his preoccupation with it. He taps a part of the something-settled matter in his heart whose threat permanently underlay his transcendental vision. The great upsurge of creative activity, Catel points out, which produced the 1855 *Leaves of Grass* partially resolved the conflicts that led to it, but only partially, "for the work of art, even if a substitute for action, does not exhaust the forces that lie in a dream-filled sleep within us" (p. 8). In "The Sleepers" these forces stir.

I must not leave this poem, however, without noting the chief fact about it, namely that these dreams *are* dreams. Their content, which I am suggesting is as real as anything in Whitman, can reach such full expression only because it does so in the guise of dreams, just as the theme of death can enter this poem with so little resistance because these dead are not dead, but sleepers merely. I have been stressing one element of the consciousness that controls this poem because it comes closest to the dark or demonic underside of Whitman's vision which I am concerned to bring out, but there is another element, strong from the beginning, which takes over after the dream sequence is over and erases its anxieties in an all-embracing consolation. This might be called the maternal element, the thought of sleep not as death or self-loss but as rest and restoration. Here certainly one cannot maintain that Whitman does not assert a belief in the future, for the poem rests for its consolation entirely on the analogy of death and night. As sleep banishes the cares that infest the day, so the dead "pass the invigoration of the night and the chemistry of the night and awake" to new life. I will not try to worry Whitman's beautiful fable into consistency with my general position, though I think it could be done, but simply note that this night-myth of restoration, like the day-myth of an unwounded wholeness that needs no restoration, is a total one. Both combine with all of the 1855 poems to celebrate life's perfection.

II

The poems of 1856 and the poems in the Valentine MSS. which Bowers[9] dates 1857 do not evidence any basic change of position. Whitman continues to affirm life and immortality, proclaims the perfection of nature, including the body and all its functions, announces his perfect happiness, and begins a systematic program of applying his affirmative insight to every aspect of the world around him. A few poems of 1857, however, strike a darker note. "I Sit and Look Out" is among this number, as are "A Hand-Mirror," "You Felons on Trial in Courts," "Of Him I Love Day and Night," and one or two more. Thoughts of guilt, evil, and death emerge in these short lyrics without any compensating affirmation except the context of other poems. We notice also that a largely 1857 poem of affirmation like "A Song of Joys" is in places more wildly exuberant, more desperately aggressive in tone than anything that had preceded it. These and other small indications suggest that the wave of confidence that crested in 1855 is beginning to falter and break of its own momentum. The blow that apparently struck the man in 1858 or 1859 precipitated a crisis in his poems and no doubt deepened it, but some crisis or other was bound to occur in any case.

For some reason, perhaps simply that Whitman was busy, no poems can be certainly dated 1858. 1859 was the Calamus year. Of the twenty-six poems in the Valentine MSS. that were probably written in 1859, twenty-two are Calamus poems, whereas almost none that can be dated earlier are clearly of this kind. The "Calamus fragrance," to use Bowers's expression, that sifts into the two program poems of the 1860 edition, "Starting From Paumanok" and "So Long," was apparently added in 1859. Add the half a dozen or so more Calamus poems that appeared in the 1860 edition, all of which may well date from 1859 also, and you have just about all the Calamus material in *Leaves of Grass*. In 1859, give or take a few months, Whitman wrote nearly all the Calamus poems he was to

[9] Fredson Bowers, *Whitman's Manuscripts:* Leaves of Grass *(1860)* (Chicago, 1955).

write and wrote little else. In view of these facts, his later contention that these poems were part of a considered program
toward which he was moving from the beginning seems highly
unlikely. Rather, something utterly unforeseen has irrupted into
his work, sweeping the rest of it aside and engrossing both man
and poet. What the source of this new thing was can be conjectured, though we do not know the biographical facts. Whitman
had some sort of unhappy love relation with a man,[10] one that
brought him a brief glimpse of happiness and then plunged him
into bitter suffering. His suffering, we may believe, was intensified
by the confirmation of his darkest suspicions about his own nature.
To someone who, like his time and place, was in many ways as
unsophisticated and even puritanical in sexual matters as Whitman
seems to have been, for all his big talk, this decisive demonstration
of his own difference came as a bewildering shock.[11]

The consequences for his poetry of this crisis are spelled out
for us in one of the three "summation" poems that came out of
this year, "As I Ebb'd With the Ocean of Life,"[12] which reads like
a conscious repudiation of "Song of Myself." The central figure
is the poet—and in early notebook drafts, as well as in the Preface,
the hero of the 1855 edition was the poet—engaged in the same
search for "types" from which he had once gathered such a rich
harvest. Nature ironically offers him the trash on the water's edge,
and with a shock of recognition he finds in it the emblem of his
present state, namely his inability any more to see saving emblems.

[10] "In spite of a few moments of happiness that Whitman may possibly have had
in a love affair [in 1858 or 1859], it is highly probable that after all _he was not talking
of any erotic relationship,_ that it never actually developed that far; moreover _I
suspect that, after all, Whitman never actually had any such experience during his
whole life, in spite of his homosexual bent_" (Schyberg-Allen, p. 167, Schyberg's
italics). See the whole passage.

[11] I am glad to acknowledge a debt here to an acute article by Clark Griffith,
"Sex and Death: The Significance of Whitman's _Calamus_ Themes," _Philological
Quarterly,_ XXXIX (1960), 18–38. While I agree with Mr. Griffith on the occasion
and the depth of Whitman's Calamus crisis, his explanation of its severity seems
to me too narrowly intellectual. It was not the mere refutation of his sex program
that devastated Whitman; it was the toppling of his entire structure of transcendental assurance.

[12] The other two being "Scented Herbage of My Breast" and "Out of the Cradle."
The order in which I discuss these poems is the one that best fits my argument.
Actually, "As I Ebb'd" was quite possibly written last, at a time when, as in "Out of
the Cradle," Whitman had reached enough perspective on his crisis to permit him
to treat it in poetry. The ebb and flow of the emotional life does not follow the tidy
patterns that are necessary for its exposition.

The poem is a farewell to his poetic vocation—premature, as it turned out, but nonetheless deeply sincere at the time. Instead of a "liberating god" and his triumphant songs of celebration, he and his "arrogant poems" are nothing, "debris." The "real Me" he thought he had courted and won in "Song of Myself" "still stands untouched, untold, altogether unreached." Instead, he is "held by the eternal self of me that threatens to get the better of me, and stifle me." He and the "Me myself" are opposed, not in union; in Melville's words, his identity has come back in horror. Now he sees the utter folly of his claim to be the master and interpreter of nature: "O I perceive I have not understood anything—not a single object—and that no man ever can." He is and always has been in the hands of mysterious great forces that save him as they please and drop him as they please.

The poem bears every mark of having been written by a man in deep grief, as indeed it was. Strangely, the whole scene is in distress and mourns with the poet even while it denies him. The wound of separation pains both alike. Its cause is mysterious, but we vaguely sense some unspecified hurt behind the vastation they lament. All we know is that the blow has been struck and he finds himself here, crushed and abandoned. The poem denies the claims of "Song of Myself" much more radically than did "The Sleepers." Whitman confronts annihilation once more, not in the guise of dreams but in waking earnest, just as if his visions of life had never been. "See! from my dead lips the ooze exuding at last!" The transcendental cycle is over. He hopes, it is true, that "the flow will return" and that he "will yet sing, someday," but this must be read as prayer, not conviction. Though he may yet in a measure recover his spirits and his singing strength, the sweeping affirmative power from which his first-phase poems had proceeded will never return in that form again.

Rather he finds a way out on the other side of his despair itself. We can watch this happen in one of the most extraordinary poems he ever wrote, "Scented Herbage of My Breast." This, like "As I Ebb'd," is another farewell to his vocation as the poet of Life—indeed, to life itself. The poet, anticipating the death he now welcomes, thinks of his "leaves," no longer as the grass growing even on graves to show "there is really no death," but as delicate "tomb-leaves" that will survive for a while the killing winter, as he cannot, to bloom perennially from his grave and tell "a few" of the suffering from which they sprang. The poem is itself a "breast leaf" of the kind it describes, a solitary cry of grief like the song of the bird in "Out of the Cradle." It soon drops its elegiac tone and speaks out directly.

> O aching and throbbing! O these hungering desires!
> Surely one day they will be pacified—all will be accomplished
> O I know not what you mean—you are not happiness—you are
>   often too bitter![13]

The interpolated assurance here, an echo of his old faith, is now purely a desperate expression of need. The true ground of his pain is the recognition that *nothing* will pacify his desires, that love is necessarily something unaccomplished. Why this must be so becomes clear when we remember what Whitman meant by love. He has been shown at last what real love is only to find that it is something that cannot and must not hope for fulfillment. Since love is also the only real thing in life, the heart of this poem is a genuinely tragic recognition: to live is to love and to love is to lose. Love is the beginning of life and also its end. Whitman has moved in this poem beyond the personal torment of such a Calamus poem as "Hours Continuing Long"* to a universal insight.

Not that "Scented Herbage" is any the less passionate for that; it is the most passionate love poem he ever wrote. His recognition lifts him to a kind of exaltation. Death becomes beautiful to him, not because it promises him the fulfillment life denies him, but simply because his love is so strong that it must go somewhere and this is the only way open to it. Since to love is to lose, "the high Soul of lovers welcomes death most." Life reserves for the lover its final secret, that the "real reality" is love and death. The poem rises to meet the new knowledge that the needs of the heart are not met by life, that man is born for defeat. The only course open to him, then, is to consent to what must be, cast off his demand for life and fear of death and go to meet his fate halfway. "Death or life I am then indifferent—my Soul declines to prefer." Its exaltation is the exaltation of passing beyond hope and illusion to a knowledge of what life and death finally are. "The readiness is all."

> He is King of Harm
> Who hath suffered Him.

---

[13] MS version, Bowers, p. 70.

*Excluded from *Leaves of Grass* after the third edition; for its text, see Blodgett and Bradley (Bibliography, below), p. 596—ED.

I have suggested that at the peak of his transcendental vision Whitman knew immortality by direct insight, with no need for the aid of myth or doctrine. Something like that is true at this second peak also. The knowledge to which this poem rises of love and death as the real reality is without intermediary or metaphor.

> Emblematic and capricious blades, I leave you—now you
>   serve me not,
> Away! I will say what I have to say, by itself. . . .

If there is such a thing as tragic Reason, then this is its poem. Death is welcomed, not because of any promise or myth, nor through mere despair of life, but simply in and for itself, because it is real.

It would be pleasant to ring down the curtain on this high note, as on one of the soaring fifth-act arias which this poem much resembles, but with thirty years of Whitman's work and at least one of his greatest poems still to come that would hardly be accurate. This kind of vision, too, like all vision, has its laws and limits. One difference between art and life is that the tragic hero can remain frozen on his peak of exaltation while the actual man must come down from such heights and go on living. Whitman, I would guess, found it much harder to hold to his tragic vision in its purity than he had found it to maintain his transcendental one. It seems likely that only an extraordinary stress of feeling brought him to the point of such vision at all; as that stress diminished he never quite reached it again, though if my thesis is correct its impact decisively controls all his later work.

A "dialectical" pattern of emotional development much like that which reached its definitive artistic expression in "When Lilacs Last," I am arguing, was a central pattern in his own experience, *lived through* by him well before he ever looked into Hegel. From the simultaneous knowledge of the ever-present immortality and of the event of death, the transcendental assurance and its demonic shadow, each dominant in turn according to the strength or weakness of his vision of safety, he moved, under the impact of his awakening to love and death, to a new knowledge both sadder and surer. If there was loss in the collapse of his total triumph over

death, there was gain in the certainty that no further shock of
awakening could come to him; now he *knew*. The ground of
the recovery which, as Asselineau argues, the very publication of the 1860 edition attests[14] was thus laid by the same
discovery that destroyed the overconfidence out of which his
poems had begun. The knowledge it brought him, the stoic
privilege it gave him of being one of those that know the truth,
became the rock on which his mature equilibrium thereafter
was founded. His wound-dressing years tested and confirmed
it but did not create it.

A similar process of confirmation can be traced in the
poems. Since it brought him at last to assurances of immortality that superficially resemble his first-phase proclamations
and which in his final philosophic phase, when he wished to
insist on the synthetic unity of his whole work, he was glad to
merge with them, it is important to insist that they do not have
the same basis. Whitman did not just "recover his serenity,"
if by that we mean that all became as it had been. The greatest
disservice the later Whitman did himself was to lead us to over-
look and belittle the significance of his deepest crisis. After he
"had been to touch the great death," he could no longer reach,
and no longer needed, the power to affirm that death did not exist.
He never again looked for final satisfaction to life, nor did he again
fall under the old terror of annihilation.

What happened instead was that he began instinctively to
build on his new insight, as he had his old, with imaginative materials, to bolster and confirm it, if also somewhat to ease it, with
"carols of death" more suitable to the needs of the Understanding.
Since metaphors for the Understanding are the lifeblood of poetry
it appears foolish to complain of this process and indeed I do not.
Many of its results, such as "Darest Thou Now, O Soul" or "Whispers of Heavenly Death" or "Reconciliation," not to mention
"When Lilacs Last," are particularly beautiful, so that one would
be grateful for Whitman's Calamus crisis if it had led to nothing
else. It is a measure of his achievement in "Scented Herbage" to
suggest that such poems are in any sense deficient by comparison.
On a level just below them is a poem like "Passage to India," one
of the best of Whitman's second-best poems, where the metaphor
has begun to shrink and harden into a relatively conventional

---

[14] *L'évolution*, p. 113; *The Evolution*, p. 114.

doctrine of the soul's immortal safety on "the seas of God" beyond the grave. We can catch this mythologizing process at its inception and perhaps at its best in "Out of the Cradle."

III

In "Out of the Cradle" Whitman has contrived to tell his whole story and even to go beyond it. The long one-sentence "pre-verse" is intended to establish the basic fiction of the poem. The poet will tell us of something long past, he suggests, which now for some reason comes over his memory. By this distancing device he contrives to win some artistic and personal control over his material. In most versions the distinction of the poet that is and the boy that was is made sharp and distinct:

> I, chanter of pains and joys, uniter of here and hereafter . . .
> A reminiscence sing.

Such a bardic line implies firm poetic control, emotion recollected in tranquillity. But neither this line nor the following one is in the 1859 version, where the poet therefore seems much more under the spell of the memories that have seized him:

> A man—yet by these tears a little boy again,
> Throwing myself on the sand, I,
> Confronting the waves, sing.

What has actually seized him, of course, is the meaning *now* to him of these images, so much so that in the first version he has a hard time keeping the presentness of his feelings from bursting through and destroying his narrative fiction.

Nevertheless, the reminiscent mode of the poem greatly enlarges its range by permitting him to bring his whole life to bear on it. As a poem of loss and awakening it goes back even to his very earliest loss and awakening, the "primal" separation of the child from the mother. Though this theme is stressed at once by the poet, especially in the original version, one must avoid reductiveness here. This layer of the poem underlies the whole and already predicts its shape, but it is not the completed structure.

From it comes, however, a powerful metaphor for the awakening that is the main subject.

The boy, leaving his bed, finds himself wandering in a strange dark world like something out of Blake, a haunted borderland between shore and sea, here and hereafter, conscious and unconscious. In its troubled restlessness it resembles the moonlit swamp that is glimpsed for a moment in "Song of Myself," or some of the dream-scenes in "The Sleepers." We sense here, especially in the 1859 version, which is more dark and troubled throughout than the final one, the same dumb, unassuageable grief as in "As I Ebb'd." It also is a wounded world, impotently twining and twisting with the pain of some obscure fatality. Here there is even less visible occasion for such agony, since the chief actor is not a broken poet but a curious child. The poem is heavy with the man's foreknowledge of what the child, now born, must go through. Like the star in "When Lilacs Last," however, the scene also has something to tell, some "drowned secret" which it is struggling to utter. It does not merely mourn a loss, like the seascape in "As I Ebb'd," but also hints of something to be found.

What has drawn the boy from his infantile security into this parturient midnight is a bird. In a flashback the poet tells of the brief May idyll of Two Together, the sudden loss of the she-bird, and the wonderful song of woe that followed, drawing the boy back night after night to listen until the night came when he awakened to its meaning. Then it seemed to him that the bird was a messenger, an interpreter, singing on behalf of the new world he had entered to tell him its secret. This secret is really two secrets, that the meaning of life is love and that he is to be its poet. The song releases the love and the songs of love in his own heart, which he now realizes has long been ready and waiting for this moment; he awakes and ecstatically dedicates himself to this service.

Yet, bewilderingly, this discovery of what life means and what he is for at once plunges him into new trouble and doubt; he finds himself once more groping for something unknown, and is not released until the voice of the sea whispers him a very different secret, the word death. This *double* awakening provides criticism with its chief problem in this poem. It is true that the boy's spiritual development is dramatically consistent and requires no explanation from outside the poem, but it is complex and rapid, an extreme example of dramatic foreshortening. Since it is also intensely personal, the biographical framework I have sketched helps to make its meaning clear.

To put the matter summarily, in the boy's awakening Whitman has fused all his own awakenings together, with the result that his poem moves in one night over a distance which he had taken forty years of life to cover. The emotional foreground, of course, is occupied by the tragic awakening of 1859, the discovery of love not merely as a passion for one particular being rather than an appetite for everything in general, but also as inherently unsatisfied. Love and grief are one. The bird's story is Whitman's story, distanced and disguised, but it is also man's. The outsetting bard of love will be the bard of unsatisfied love because there is no other kind.

But here we encounter a difficulty, for in many of the other poems of 1859 Whitman had suggested that his awakening to love had stopped his poems and ended his poetic career. Of course he could hardly have overlooked the fact that his crisis did arouse him to new poems and to some of his best. Certainly he was proud of this poem, immediately printed it and followed it with one of his self-written reviews announcing that he would not be mute any more. Perhaps we may read a special meaning into his selection of this poem as the first public evidence of his return to song. In this "reminiscence" of the birth of his poetic vocation he is actually celebrating its recovery. The process of relieving his pain in song has now proceeded so far, past "death's outlet" songs like "Hours Continuing Long" and "As I Ebb'd," past a poem of first recognition like "Scented Herbage," that he can now begin to see that the deathblow to his old "arrogant poems" is proving to be a lifeblow to new and better if more sorrowful ones, and so for the first time, in the guise of a reminiscence, he can make not just his grief, but its transmutation into the relief of song the subject of his singing.

In the measure that he recovers his poetic future he also recovers his past. His sense of returning powers naturally picks up and blends with his memories of that other awakening, whenever and whatever it was, that led to the poems of 1855. In the boy's joy he draws on and echoes his first awakening, the ecstatic union of self and soul celebrated in "Song of Myself," when he *had* felt a thousand songs starting to life within him in response to the "song of Two Together." Overlaid on that is his second dark awakening to the truth of "two together no more" which had at first

appeared to end his singing. If we thus provisionally disentangle
the strands that Whitman has woven together we can understand
better why the song of the bird must plunge the boy almost simultaneously into ecstasy and despair.

The steps of this process are obscured for us in the final version by Whitman's deletion of a crucial stanza that explains why
the boy needs a word from the sea when he already has so much
from the bird. After the lines

> O give me some clue!
> O if I am to have so much, let me have more!

the original version continued as follows:

> O a word! O what is my destination?
> O I fear it is henceforth chaos!
> O how joys, dreads, convolutions, human shapes, and all shapes,
>   spring as from graves around me!
> O phantoms! You cover all the land and all the sea!
> O I cannot see in the dimness whether you smile or frown
>   upon me!
> O vapor, a look, a word! O well-beloved!
> O you dear women's and men's phantoms!

This stanza or something similar appears in all editions of "Out
of the Cradle" until the last version of 1881, when Whitman was
twenty years away from his poem. Perhaps he dropped it then because he felt it spoke too plainly from the emotions of 1859 and
was not in keeping with what his poem had become. That it was
not necessary to the success of the poem is proved by the success
the poem has had without it, yet its omission greatly changes the
total effect. The quality of the boy's need is lightened to a more
usual adolescent distress and the sea's answer becomes the kind
of grave reassurance characteristic of the later Whitman. In the
original version the boy is not just distressed, he is desperate with
the desperation of the man of 1859. The first act of his awakened
poet's vision has been to abort and produce a frightening chaos.
Instead of the triumphant vision of Life which Whitman himself
had known, when the whole world smiled on its conquering lover,
nothing rises now before the outsetting bard but a dim phantas-
magoria of death-shapes. It is almost impossible not to read this
passage as coming from the poet himself rather than from the boy

—indeed, Whitman was right to cut it, it *is* out of keeping—for these "dear women's and men's phantoms" are surely dear because they are those of the men and women and the whole world that had *already* started to life for him in his poems, their life the eddying of his living soul, but are now strengthless ghosts, like the power of vision from which their life had come. This is the "terrible doubt of appearances" that had plagued him from the beginning, now revived and confirmed by his new crisis. Whitman here openly transfers to the boy the man's despair.

With this background it should not be hard to see that the answer the sea gives to the despair characteristic of 1859 is the answer characteristic of 1859. Its essential quality is the same tragic acceptance as in "Scented Herbage," a knowledge of death not as consolation or promise, still less as mere appearance, but as reality, the "real reality" that completes the reality of love in the only way in which it can be completed. In the language of Thoreau, the sea is a "realometer" that says, "this is, and no mistake." The lift her answer brings is like that of "Scented Herbage," the lift of naming the whole truth and so passing beyond illusion to a consent to fate. A sign that this is so is the sea's taciturnity. The thrush's beautiful song of death in 1865, weaving a veil of life-illusion over the same hard truth and so easing it for us, is not present here; simply the word, the thing itself. In this stark directness, again, the kinship is to "Scented Herbage" rather than to "When Lilacs Last."

Yet certainly the fact that this word also, like the bird's song of love and the boy's despair, is ascribed to a dramatic character makes a profound difference. The sea as dramatic character in this poem has two phases. In the earlier part, before the boy turns to her for his answer, she is a background voice blending with the drama of bird and boy but essentially not a part of it. She has an ancient sorrow of her own which leaves her no grief to spare for this small incident on her shores. She does not share the egocentric fallacy of boy and bird, in which even moon, wind, and shadows join in futile sympathy. In this part of the poem she is the same sea as in "As I Ebb'd," the "fierce old mother" who "endlessly cries for her castaways"—all her castaways, not just these—the deep ocean of life and death that rolls through all things.

Of course, behind every detail of the poem, including this one, we feel the poet's shaping power, creating a symbolical language for the life of his own mind. In this kind of subjective drama the author is all the characters; bird, boy, and sea are one and join in a grief that is at bottom the same because it is his own. But Whitman has now seen through the Emersonian illusion that the power of the poet prophesies a victory for the man. Where "Song of Myself" had dramatized the omnipotence of bardic vision, "Out of the Cradle" dramatizes the discovery that the power of the bard is only to sing his own limits. Like the bird in Marianne Moore's poem, his singing is mighty because he is caged. As a dramatic character, then, the sea is the Not-Me, Fate, Karma, that-which-cannot-be-changed. As such she dominates the scene, which is all, as Kenneth Burke would say, under her aegis, but she does not share in its temporal passions.

At the end, however, she condescends to reveal herself and changes from the ground of the question to the answer. The change is not so much in the sea as in the boy. As before, he hears when he is ready to listen; the sea has been speaking all the time. Even the bird, in the early version, heard her and responded with continued song. Before he can hear her the boy must finish his egocentric cycle and pass from his hybristic promise to sing "clearer, louder, and more sorrowful" songs than the bird's to his despairing recognition that there is no good in him. The sign that he is ready is the question itself. Then the sea approaches and whispers as privately for him, revealing the secret which will release him from passion to perception. What she shows him is, I have suggested, no consoling revelation but simply reality. Yet the fact that this answer is now felt to come from the sea, from the heart of the Not-Me that has defeated Whitman's arrogant demands for another Me, suggests that the division between him and his world is not final after all, that the separation both have suffered can still be healed. The elemental forces of "As I Ebb'd" have fused with the perception of reality in "Scented Herbage" to form a new Thou, in Buber's language—no longer the tousled mistress Whitman had ordered around in "Song of Myself," certainly, but a goddess who will speak to him when he is ready to accept her on her own terms. Then he can hear in the voice of the sea the voice of a mother, a figure as we know "always near and always divine" to him. The real reality of "Scented Herbage" has acquired a local habitation and a name, has gathered around itself life and numenosity, and Whitman is well on his way by this dark path to replace the Comrade who had deserted him on the open road.

James E. Miller, Jr.

Walt Whitman and the Modern Image

> The force that through the green fuse drives the
> flower
> Drives my green age.
>
> —*Dylan Thomas*

Walt Whitman has always seemed to evoke from his passionate readers responses remarkable in their intensity. From the fanatic loyalty of W. D. O'Connor, who wrote *The Good Gray Poet*, to the deep-seated revulsion of John Greenleaf Whittier, who threw his copy of the 1855 edition of *Leaves of Grass* into the fire, few poets have elicited such impassioned gestures of approval or disapproval from their readers.

The history of Whitman's reputation is filled with fascinating accounts of passionate attachments, explosive reprovals, denials, and reversals. So much smoke has been produced by the heated controversies that it has been almost impossible to see distinctly what fed the flames. But it has always been clear that the passions of the participants have been deeply and directly involved.

A re-examination of the startlingly varied responses to Whitman of a select few nineteenth-century poets, together with a close look at the odd, seemingly irrational responses of a number of twentieth-century poets, might reveal, in some small measure at least, that enigmatic element in *Leaves of Grass* which has both attracted and repelled with such radical force. In tracking this element, we shall, perhaps, discover what one responsible and perceptive reader called the lost secret of history.

I. THE MODERN IMAGE

Although Whitman warned against movements in his name, he has been repeatedly hailed as a symbolic leader and sometime saint. The most recent canonization has taken place in San Francisco, where the high priests of the beat generation have issued their manifestoes, read their poetry to jazz, and muttered their enigmas into their cool cups.

The celebrated poet of this beat generation is Allen Ginsberg, whose book, like Whitman's, became involved with the law over alleged obscenities. There are additional and deeper resemblances. We are told that Ginsberg's book was first to have been called *Yawp!,* after Whitman's primitive outcry in "Song of Myself," but that instead the beat poet finally settled on *Howl!* His instinct was right. His poems are not so much a barbaric yawp as an agonizing howl.

Ginsberg's specific tribute to Whitman appears in a short poem, "A Supermarket in California" (dated 1955), which opens:

> What thoughts I have of you tonight, Walt Whitman, for I walked down the sidestreets under the trees with a headache self-conscious looking at the full moon.
> In my hungry fatigue, and shopping for images, I went into the neon fruit supermarket, dreaming of your enumerations!
> What peaches and what penumbras! Whole families shopping at night! Aisles full of husbands! Wives in the avocados, babies in the tomatoes!—and you, Garcia Lorca, what were you doing down by the watermelons?
>
> I saw you, Walt Whitman, childless, lonely old grubber, poking among the meats in the refrigerator and eyeing the grocery boys.
> I heard you asking questions of each: Who killed the pork chops? What price bananas? Are you my Angel?[1]

[1] Allen Ginsberg, *Howl!* (San Francisco: The City Lights Pocket Bookshop, 1956). pp. 23–24.

The lines recall, in a bizarre way, Whitman's line in "Song of Myself"—"I reach to the leafy lips, I reach to the polish'd breasts of melons." There is, running through the Ginsberg lines, as through many of the most brilliant passages of Whitman, a sexual symbolism and sexual identification that seems constantly on the verge of becoming embarrassingly explicit. In spite of the image of Whitman as the "lonely old grubber," Ginsberg's portrait of the poet ("dear father, graybeard, lonely old courage-teacher") is basically sympathetic, and as they wander (in Ginsberg's poetic imagination) out of the supermarket into the night, they seem drawn together in a lonely communion derived from a secret understanding: they "stroll dreaming of the lost America of love."

Ginsberg's image of Whitman is a far cry from the image of the Good Gray Poet, or of the Poet of Democracy, or of the Singer of America. But the beat generation was not the first to envision an off-beat image of Whitman. Dylan Thomas, in a poem only recently published (in *Letters to Vernon Watkins,* 1957) but contained in a 19 March 1940 letter, sketches an unusual Whitman. Thomas explains in his letter: "I've got very little to say about it [the poem] myself: you'll see the heavy hand with which I make fun of this middle-class beardless Walt who props humanity, in his dirty, weeping, expansive moments, against corners & counters & tries to slip, in grand delusions of all embracing humanitarianism, everyone into himself." In the poem ("The Countryman's Return"), Whitman's long line with its majestic sweep of all-inclusiveness is reduced to an absurd brevity and Whitman's ecstatically sung catalogue is turned into a halting and niggling list of the ludicrous:

> Beggars, robbers, inveiglers,
> Voices from manholes and drains,
> Maternal short time pieces,
> Octopuses in doorways,
> Dark inviters to keyholes
> And evenings with great danes,
> Bedsitting girls on the beat
> With nothing for the metre,
> Others whose single beds hold two
> Only to make two ends meet,
> All the hypnotised city's
> Insidious procession
> Hawking for money and pity
> Among the hardly possessed.

Thomas is not writing a parody of Whitman so much as a parody of himself imitating Whitman: "And I . . . /Conjured me to resemble / A singing Walt." This singing Walt does bear some resemblance to Ginsberg's Walt poking among the pork chops at the supermarket: both Whitmans are reduced considerably in size and rendered less mythic, more human. Indeed, Thomas's identification with the poet, like Ginsberg's communion, suggests an intimacy which the reader can observe but cannot share. Thomas, too, seems to have his secret with Walt, a secret which runs much deeper than the jumbled surface of his poem.

A comparable tone of intimacy, which seems to derive from similar depths of secret familiarity, is found in the Spanish poet Federico Garcia Lorca's "Ode to Walt Whitman" (a part of his *Poet in New York,* written in 1929–30).[2] We do not read far into this modern vision of a spiritually desolate city before we discover a Whitman of extraordinary attributes:

> Not for one moment, Walt Whitman, comely old man,
> have I ceased to envision your beard full of butterflies,
> your corduroy shoulders, worn thin by the moon,
> your chaste, Apollonian thighs,
> your voice like a pillar of ashes;
> patriarch, comely as mist,
> you cried like a bird
> whose sex is transfixed by a needle;
> satyr's antagonist,
> grapevine's antagonist,
> and lover of bodies under the nap of the cloth.

With his "beard full of butterflies," his "chaste, Apollonian thighs," and his "transfixed" sex, Whitman is the symbol of agonized purity opposed in the poem to the "perverts of the cities," the "mothers of filthiness, harpies, sleeplessly thwarting / the Love that apportions us garlands of pleasure." As the poem increases in bitter condemnation of the perverts and "toadies," it increases in intensity of shared feeling with "handsome Walt Whitman." As in Ginsberg's and Thomas's Whitman, there seem to be lurking in Lorca's image of the poet enigmatic qualities which only Lorca fully and sympathetically comprehends.

Hart Crane, in the "Cape Hatteras" section of *The Bridge* (1930), may seem on first glance to present a more conventional

[2] Federico Garcia Lorca, *Poet in New York,* trans. Ben Belitt (New York: Grove Press, 1955), pp. 118–127.

Whitman than Lorca's, Thomas's, or Ginsberg's. Crane seems to invoke Whitman as his and the nation's creative daemon or divinity:

> Our Meistersinger, thou set breath in steel;
> And it was thou who on the boldest heel
> Stood up and flung the span on even wing
> Of that great Bridge, our Myth, whereof I sing!

But this "national" Whitman is not the conventional, yawping American chauvinist; he is the maker of a complex myth of possible future fulfillment. A note of intimacy is introduced early in "Cape Hatteras":

> Or to read you, Walt—knowing us in thrall
> To that deep wonderment, our native clay
> Whose depth of red, eternal flesh of Pocahontus . . .

Basic to Whitman's myth (as delineated by Crane) is his sexual insight into man's thralldom to his "native clay," a fundamental element of man's nature celebrated elsewhere in *The Bridge* in the figure of Pocahontus as emblem of the eternal female principle. But also basic to the myth is Whitman's spiritual insight into man's adhesive attachment to his comrade, the Whitman of "Recorders Ages Hence" in "Calamus." Crane continues in "Cape Hatteras":

> . . . in pure impulse inbred
> To answer deepest soundings! O, upward from the dead
> Thou bringest tally, and a pact, new bound,
> Of living brotherhood!

Though Crane's Whitman is elevated to a national mythmaker, he is not inflated into a gaseous, windy orator. Indeed, that suggestion of a complex vision intuitively shared, present in Ginsberg, Lorca, and Thomas, runs through all Crane's lines, including the closing:

> Yes, Walt,
> Afoot again, and onward without halt—
> Not soon, nor suddenly—No, never to let go
>   My hand
>   in yours,
>   Walt Whitman—
>   so—

II. THE BEWILDERING RESPONSE

Crane, Thomas, Lorca, and Ginsberg all participate in the creation of a twentieth-century Walt Whitman who was relatively
unknown in the nineteenth. This lonely old grubber, with butterflies in his beard, expansively singing as he strolls hand in hand
with his comrade-poets, is something of an eccentric and an
exile—but mystically appealing and containing unplumbed depths
of human understanding.

During Whitman's own time, two images of him warred with
each other, neither ever quite firmly established, but both so
strongly asserted that subtle composites or radically new charac-
terizations seemed impossible. The poet's friends and the poet
himself promulged the image of the Good Gray Poet—an image
so inhumanly pure and innocent that even Whitman's strongest
twentieth-century admirers reject it. The poet's enemies, abetted
by the tight-lipped disapproval of the genteel tradition, painted a
picture of sexual indecency and moral depravity that can only
draw a smile from the sophisticated modern reader.

The nineteenth century's insistence on a Whitman absolutely
pure or totally depraved resulted in some curious and revealing
incidents in the erratic growth of the poet's reputation. As there
was no middle ground to which to retreat, nineteenth-century
readers, when they did not simply ignore Whitman, usually became deeply involved, either as disciple or enemy. Some, like
W. D. O'Connor and Horace Traubel, made up the band of hot
little prophets that seemed to fight for Whitman's deification.
Others, who generally preferred the anonymity of such organiza-
tions as Anthony Comstock's Society for the Suppression of Vice,
denounced, sometimes violently, the obscenity of both the poet
and his book.

In the midst of this strange struggle, it should not be surprising
to find curious ambivalences and even sudden reversals in the
nineteenth-century response to Whitman. Many commentaries
could be cited, but three important ones should suffice to illustrate
the pattern: those of Ralph Waldo Emerson, Sidney Lanier, and
Algernon C. Swinburne. Each of these writers reacted to Whitman
in a special way. Emerson's initial enthusiastic letter was followed
by a long silence. Lanier attempted to explain the conflict in his
emotional and intellectual response. Swinburne began in adulation
and ended in vilification.

In many ways Emerson's brief letter,[3] properly titled the most significant letter in American literature, contains some of the most astute criticism of Whitman ever written, and it was apparently dashed off in the first flush of a strong, sympathetic response to that 1855 edition: "I am very happy in reading [*Leaves of Grass*], as great power makes us happy. . . . I give you joy of your free and brave thought. . . . I find the courage of treatment which so delights us, and which large perception only can inspire. . . . the solid sense of the book is a sober certainty." *Solid sense, courage of treatment, free and brave thought*—these are not the casual phrases of a polite thank-you note, but the profound tribute of a deep, spontaneous impression. Whatever the ethics involved in Whitman's unauthorized use of the letter to publicize his book, Whitman was certainly right in gauging the success of his poetry by this one intelligent and unsolicited reaction. Emerson's closing sentence—"I wish to see my benefactor, and have felt much like striking my tasks and visiting New York to pay you my respects" —suggests that same desire to stroll hand in hand expressed by Crane and Ginsberg. Indeed, that personal note of intimate and even exhilarated understanding dominates Emerson's letter. The reason for Emerson's subsequent silence, even to the exclusion of Whitman from his 1874 anthology of American poetry, will probably remain obscure. But we may guess that Emerson felt the Victorian necessity of atoning for the "sin" of this one indecent exposure of his raw, instinctive response. The feelings called forth by Whitman's powerful poetry might prove troublesome, even if one attempted to clothe their nakedness in the garments of gentility.

Sidney Lanier, in a confession of his honest response to *Leaves of Grass,* began with a staggering series of qualifications which Emerson probably wished he had made in his 1855 letter—and which he might have made had he expected publication. But Lanier apparently felt the strong necessity of bringing his imprecise emotional involvement into some kind of intellectual focus, and as a result tripped himself up in one of the oddest—and funniest—commentaries ever made on Whitman:

> Here let me first carefully disclaim and condemn all that flippant and sneering tone which dominates so many discussions of Whitman.

[3] *The Poetry and Prose of Walt Whitman: with a biographical introduction and a basic selection of early and recent critical commentary,* ed. Louis Untermeyer (New York: Simon and Schuster, 1949), pp. 963–964.

> While I differ from him utterly as to every principle of artistic pro-
> cedure; while he seems to me the most stupendously mistaken man in
> all history as to what constitutes true democracy, and the true ad-
> vance of art and man; while I am immeasurably shocked at the sweep-
> ing invasions of those reserves which depend on the very personality
> I have so much insisted upon, and which the whole consensus of the
> ages has considered more and more sacred with every year of growth
> in delicacy; yet, after all these prodigious allowances, I owe some
> keen delights to a certain combination of bigness and naïvety which
> makes some of Whitman's passages so strong and taking, and, indeed,
> on the one occasion when Whitman has abandoned his theory of
> formlessness and written in form he has made *My Captain, O My
> Captain* [*sic*] surely one of the most tender and beautiful poems in
> any language.[4]

Surely very few paragraphs in all of criticism begin with such a
bang and end with such a whimper. After the considerable build-
up to Whitman's *bigness and naïvety,* we are offered not a "strong
and taking" example—possibly one of those "sweeping invasions"
—but the flat and jingling *My Captain, O My Captain:* the very
mistitling suggests the violent application of the brakes on an
untraveled sideroad and a sudden return to the public highway.
But in spite of Lanier's shifting directions, he gives us a momentary
glimpse, in acknowledging "some keen delights," of a personal
Whitman related to Emerson's or Ginsberg's.

   Unlike Emerson, Swinburne wrote his first, enthusiastic praise
of Whitman for publication. In his essay on Blake, Swinburne
selected Whitman as the measure of comparison:

> The points of contact and sides of likeness between William
> Blake and Walt Whitman are so many and so grave, as to afford some
> ground of reason to those who preach the transition of souls or trans-
> fusion of spirits. The great American is not a more passionate
> preacher of sexual or political freedom than the English artist. . . .
> To each all sides and shapes of life are alike acceptable or endurable.
> From the fresh free ground of either workman nothing is excluded
> that is not exclusive. The words of either strike deep and run wide
> and soar high.[5]

This bold, daring praise, with emphasis on the *fresh free ground,*
the deep striking and the high soaring, recalls the exhilarated re-

---

[4] Sidney Lanier, *The English Novel,* ed. Clarence Gohdes and Kemp Malone
(Baltimore: The Johns Hopkins Press, 1945), p. 39.
   [5] See note 3, above, p. 996.

sponse of Emerson and the reluctant response of Lanier. But Swinburne adds a touch of casual defiance in his admiration for the *passionate preacher of sexual freedom*. These words must have burned in his mind when, some twenty years later, Swinburne in "Whitmania" recanted with the same intense energy of his earlier praise.

> But under the dirty clumsy paws of a harper whose plectrum is a muck-rake any tune will become a chaos of discords. . . . Mr. Whitman's Eve is a drunken apple-woman, indecently sprawling in the slush and garbage of the gutter amid the rotten refuse of her overturned fruit-stall . . . Mr. Whitman's Venus is a Hottentot wench under the influence of cantharides and adulterated rum.[6]

Twenty years can make a lot of difference, especially in one's sexual views. But there seems to be an unreasoned hostility, perhaps based on fear, in Swinburne's vitriolic attack. We can only exclaim with Whitman (when he was informed of Swinburne's switch from prophet to enemy), "Ain't he the damndest simulacrum."

III. VIRGINS, DYNAMOS, AND SEX

In reading Emerson, Lanier, and Swinburne, we recognize, if but fleetingly, a common ground with Crane, Lorca, Thomas, and Ginsberg. But the chasm that separates the previous age from the present cannot be easily bridged.

In search of a link, we might well begin with a nineteenth-century figure who lived on into the twentieth. Henry Adams's search for the secret of history took him far beyond both of the centuries in which he lived. But it was the powerful dynamo of his own industrial age that gave him the clue he sought. The clue led back to the thirteenth-century Virgin. Having identified history as sequence, Adams examined and rejected in turn the sequence of men, the sequence of society, the sequence of time, the sequence of thought. He came around finally to the sequence of force, which yielded a logical connection between the thirteenth century's Virgin and the nineteenth century's Dynamo.

Upon discovering this connection, Adams next raised the question of sex as force:

[6] *Ibid.*, p. 1005.

. . . any one brought up among Puritans knew that sex was sin. In any previous age, sex was strength. Neither art nor beauty was needed. Every one, even among Puritans, knew that neither Diana of the Ephesians nor any of the Oriental goddesses was worshipped for her beauty. She was goddess because of her force; she was the animated dynamo; she was reproduction—the greatest and most mysterious of all energies; all she needed was to be fecund.

Observing in passing the significant creative link between Lucretius's invocation of Venus and Dante's invocation of the Virgin, Adams turned finally to the American mind and American art (he refers to himself in his *Education* in the third person):

On one side, at the Louvre and at Chartres [art and architecture inspired by the Madonna], as he knew by the record of work actually done and still before his eyes, was the highest energy ever known to man, the creator of four-fifths of his noblest art, exercising vastly more attraction over the human mind than all the steam-engines and dynamos ever dreamed of; and yet this energy was unknown to the American mind. An American Virgin would never dare command; an American Venus would never dare exist. . . . Adams began to ponder, asking himself whether he knew of any American artist who had ever insisted on the power of sex, as every classic had always done; but he could think only of Walt Whitman. . . . All the rest had used sex for sentiment, never for force.[7]

There seems to be, in this one casual reference to Whitman, more revealed insight than in many a full treatise on the poet. Whitman emerges as neither the Good Gray Poet nor an obscene old man, but as the poet of sexual force, the poet of procreation. It was this fresh wind blowing through his *Leaves* that Emerson and Lanier and Swinburne felt but could not or would not identify. It is this enduring, magnetic energy in his work that constitutes the secret shared by Crane, Lorca, Thomas, and Ginsberg.

As Adams speculated on the relevance of the sexual force to history, Sigmund Freud explored the central significance of the force in the psyche, and, later, Alfred Kinsey discovered the intricate omnipresence of the force in society. It is time that criticism caught up with history and evaluated Whitman not with nineteenth-century reticence but with twentieth-century reality —a reality he prophetically anticipated.

[7] Henry Adams, *The Education of Henry Adams* (Boston: Houghton Mifflin Company, 1918), pp. 384–385.

If, as Adams suggests, *Leaves of Grass* is one of those rare classics containing the lost secret of history, Whitman's sexual vision might well come under a fresh and frank scrutiny. Though that vision comes into precise focus in the "Children of Adam" cluster, where Whitman declares himself singer of "the song of procreation," it pervades the whole of *Leaves of Grass* so as to become impossible of disentanglement from the book's total meaning. If by some intricate method the sexual content of *Leaves* were to be expurgated, the book would lie maimed and impotent before us, its strength and its vitality obliterated. As well castrate a man as bowdlerize *Leaves of Grass.*

Whitman envisioned man's sexual energy as primal, creative energy, a simple extension of a creatively evolving natural world. When Whitman loafed at his ease and observed a spear of summer grass, he saw more than an isolated green blade. He saw himself and the grass impelled to growth and reproduction by an identical creative force. Whitman repeatedly dramatized the natural world in sexual terms, constantly exploring the intimate kinship of nature and man. Such subtly sexual lines recur throughout *Leaves:*

> Smile O voluptuous cool-breath'd earth!
> Earth of the slumbering and liquid trees!
> Earth of departed sunset—earth of the mountains misty-topt!
> Earth of the vitreous pour of the full moon just tinged with
>   blue!

Indeed, Whitman might best be described as a "sexual pantheist," envisioning the world and man as infused by an identical, creative sexual vitality.

Whitman's sexual vision was comprehensive and shaped the opening sections (after the introductory cluster and poem) of *Leaves:* "Song of Myself," "Children of Adam," and "Calamus." These poems give *Leaves of Grass* its substantial sexual foundation. Freud later was to identify the three sexual stages of man as auto-, homo-, and heterosexual. Whitman has reversed the order of these last two stages, probably for programmatic purposes: he dramatizes in succession the relationship of man to self, of man to woman, of man to man: identity, love, and friendship.

Invariably in Whitman's sexual vision the physical vitality is prelude to the spiritual. The sexual awakening or the achievement of sexual identity comes in the middle of "Song of Myself," in the celebrated passage on touch, which appears largely autoerotic:

> Is this then a touch? quivering me to a new identity,
> Flames and ether making a rush for my veins,
> Treacherous tip of me reaching and crowding to help them,
> My flesh and blood playing out lightning to strike what is
>   hardly different from myself,
> On all sides prurient provokers stiffening my limbs,
> Straining the udder of my heart for its withheld drip. . . .

This passage continues developing in intensity until, with the cry, "Unclench your floodgates," a climax is reached, followed by the calm retrospect and a return to the poem's dominant image: "I believe a leaf of grass is no less than the journey-work of the stars." This entire passage represents the marvelous achievement of sexual identity through experiencing directly the sense of touch. This development of an acute physical self-consciousness is, in the poem's drama, one of the major stages on the way to spiritual identity and the mystic merge.

In "Children of Adam" Whitman turns from man alone to man and woman. The poems of this cluster were to "Celebrate you act divine and you children prepared for, / And you stalwart loins." In one of these poems of procreation, "I Sing the Body Electric," the sexual drama is extended to the rhythmical flow of time itself:

> Ebb stung by the flow and flow stung by the ebb, love-flesh
>   swelling and deliciously aching,
> Limitless limpid jets of love hot and enormous, quivering jelly
>   of love, white-blow and delirious juice,
> Bridegroom night of love working surely and softly into the
>   prostrate dawn,
> Undulating into the willing and yielding day,
> Lost in the cleave of the clasping and sweet-flesh'd day.

The vivid celebrations of heterosexual love in "Children of Adam" are accompanied by an insistence throughout on the spiritual innocence of the physical act. "I Sing the Body Electric" concludes: "O I say these are not the parts and poems of the body only, but of the soul, / O I say now these are the soul!" The dominant metaphor of the cluster of poems, suggested by the title, is the Garden. The poet calls for a return to the innocent sexual existence of Adam and Eve in Eden before the Fall.

From man-woman love in "Children of Adam" Whitman turns finally to man-man love in "Calamus," pairing, as many essayists (including Emerson) had done before him, his concept of love with his concept of friendship. And like previous writers relating these two themes, Whitman uses some of the same terms of passion for the two relationships. He is concerned with drawing a clear distinction:

> Fast-anchor'd eternal O love! O woman I love!
> O bride! O wife! more resistless than I can tell, the thought
>   of you!
> Then separate, as disembodied or another born,
> Ethereal, the last athletic reality, my consolation,
> I ascend, I float in the regions of your love O man,
> O sharer of my roving life.

The "Calamus" cluster may be interpreted variously as a homosexual proclamation, a confession, an inadvertent revelation, or a sublimation—depending on one's psychoanalytical bent. But the poems' intensity of emotion strikes home as entirely honest. And the intensity is matched by an impressive breadth. Whitman ranges from the complexity of the single relationship to the vision of a democratic brotherhood based on a multiplicity of such relationships. In these poems Whitman explores and celebrates friendship in all its democratic possibilities and religious implications—as well as its Freudian subtleties.

No poet before Whitman had been so bold or so deep in his insight into the sexual intricacies of man. In vividly dramatizing the emotional complexity of man's sexual nature, Whitman was bound, naturally, both to attract and to repel. Hence that ambivalence in such nineteenth-century readers as Emerson, Lanier, and Swinburne—drawn by the fresh honesty of the vision, but frightened by its naive boldness. Sensitive twentieth-century readers, like Crane, Lorca, Thomas, and Ginsberg, have taken the honesty and the boldness as their private secret. They respond to the emotional validity of the sexual vision and accept that personal invitation to intimacy that seems to emanate from every page of *Leaves of Grass*.

Whitman was one of those "Beginners" he so knowingly described—"How dear and dreadful they are to the earth . . . / How people respond to them, yet know them not." After Whitman, the sexual force achieved solid recognition in clinic and laboratory through the investigations of such imaginative scientists as Freud and Kinsey. It came to play a central role, too, in a considerable body of literature produced by some major talents—notably Lawrence and Joyce. One wonders, even, what obscure debt Vladimir Nabokov and his nymphet owe to that lonely old Beginner, Walt Whitman.

At the end of his poetic career, in "A Backward Glance O'er Travel'd Roads," Whitman reaffirmed the sexual bias of his book: "'Leaves of Grass' is avowedly the song of Sex. . . . the espousing principle of those lines so gives breath of life to my whole scheme that the bulk of the pieces might as well have been left unwritten were those lines omitted. . . . the lines I allude to, and the spirit in which they are spoken, permeate all 'Leaves of Grass,' and the work must stand or fall with them. . . ." Whitman surely knew, as Henry Adams recognized, that in his sexual vision he had focused on a neglected historical force that was central to the human experience.

Arthur Golden

Whitman's Revisions in the Blue Book, *His Annotated Copy of the 1860 (Third) Edition of* Leaves of Grass

On 30 June 1865 Secretary of the Interior James Harlan, an unreconstructed product of the Bible Belt, dismissed Walt Whitman from his clerkship in the Indian Bureau for being the author of the notorious *Leaves of Grass*. A week before he was sworn in as Secretary, he complained to a friend that "I would much prefer to remain the residue of my term of two years in the Senate . . . than to serve in the Cabinet. Nothing but a sense of public duty would induce me to change. There is . . . a pressing necessity for a renovation in the Interior Department which may possibly control my decision, contrary to my own personal wishes." Two weeks later the essentials of his program, which have a curiously modern ring, were given in the press:

> The Secretary of the Interior has issued a circular to the heads of bureaus in the department, to report as to the loyalty of each of the employees under him, and also whether there are any whose fidelity to duty or moral character is such as to justify an immediate dispensation of their services.

Of Whitman's loyalty to the Union there could have been no question, and his fidelity to duty had been rewarded with a pro-

Reprinted by permission of the New York Public Library from The Bulletin of the New York Public Library, *69 (May 1965), 283–306. Copyright © 1965 by the New York Public Library. (Original title: "New Light on Leaves of Grass: Whitman's Annotated Copy of the 1860 (Third) Edition." This essay has been revised by the author.)*

motion several days before Harlan took office. This leaves us with Whitman's moral character, where we are on much shakier ground. In later years Harlan said he dismissed Whitman for reasons of economy, but his memory was playing tricks on him. No doubt he had inherited from the previous Secretary a lot of men he didn't need, but he had also told J. Hubley Ashton, the Assistant Attorney General who had attempted to intercede with him on Whitman's behalf, that his perusal of Whitman's personal, annotated copy of the 1860 edition of *Leaves of Grass* led directly to his dismissing the poet.[1] At no point during this interview had he mentioned to Ashton anything about the matter of economy.

How Harlan got to this copy, which Whitman was revising in preparation for the next (1867) edition and which he kept in his desk in the Indian Office, is not known. Whitman himself has reasonably suggested that a fellow clerk, glancing through this odd-looking book and recognizing at once that its contents made it a pressing case for the Secretary of the Interior, so informed Harlan, who came to Whitman's office after hours, as he told Ashton, and examined the *Blue Book*.

Ashton got Walt a job in the Attorney General's Office the very next day. Now under his protection and apparently not overworked, Whitman was able here, as Ashton put it, "to bring out with comfort to himself" the fourth edition of *Leaves,* containing many of the revisions he had initially incorporated in the *Blue Book,* and other works, including *Sequel to Drum-Taps* (1865–66), *Songs Before Parting,* the fifth edition of *Leaves of Grass* (1871–72), *Passage to India,* and *Democratic Vistas.* He stayed on in the Attorney General's Office until 1873, when he suffered a paralytic stroke and left government service to take up residence in Camden, New Jersey.

Some five months after Whitman's dismissal, his good friend William D. O'Connor, in his tract *The Good Gray Poet: A Vindication,* laced into Harlan and quite properly emphasized Whitman's kinship with other great writers of the past who had faced up to life and sex in adult terms. O'Connor also stressed Whitman's importance as a distinctly American poet. What was wrong with O'Connor's defense was that he had some difficulty in dis-

---

[1] Called the *Blue Book* because it still retains its original blue wrappers, it is in the Oscar Lion-Whitman Collection in the New York Public Library. References to this volume cited below are to *Walt Whitman's Blue Book:* Vol. I, *Facsimile;* Vol. II, *Textual Analysis,* ed. Arthur Golden (New York: New York Public Library, 1968).

tinguishing Walt Whitman from Jesus Christ; and in fact this rather one-sided view of so complex a figure has plagued Whitman scholarship until quite recently.

The Harlan-Whitman episode and the emphasis Whitman's followers had put on the sex business apparently led Oscar L. Triggs, who prepared the variorum edition of *Leaves* for the 1902 edition of the *Complete Writings* and others after him to make the assumption that Whitman had actually *suppressed* sexual passages appearing in the 1860 edition. In the 1867 edition, Triggs wrote, "Certain rough terms and many references to sexuality disappear" (Vol. X, 156), an entirely inaccurate observation, as a comparison of such passages in the third and fourth editions demonstrates.[2]

Whitman gave the *Blue Book* to Horace Traubel, one of his literary executors, in 1890, and Traubel attempted over the years to raise money to bring out a facsimile edition, but nothing came of it and the project was shelved with his death in 1919. The noted Whitman collector Oscar Lion bought the *Blue Book* in 1933 from Traubel's widow, and when in 1953 Mr. Lion gave to the New York Public Library his outstanding Whitman collection, the *Blue Book* found its final home. A gift by Mr. Lion has made possible the publication of the *Facsimile* of the *Blue Book* and the accompanying *Textual Analysis*.

I

Whitman's own comment in the Preface to *November Boughs* (1888) on the impact of the Civil War on his poetry is worth noting: "Without those three or four years and the experiences they gave, 'Leaves of Grass' would not now be existing." The 1867 edition was crucial to the direction that *Leaves of Grass* was to take, thematically, not because of any great variety of new poems he included here—there were only six[3]—but because it was in this edition, worked out of the *Blue Book,* that he explored to the fullest the theme of nationalism that he was so preoccupied with during the war.

Certainly any meaningful assessment of Whitman's poetry

---

[2] For supporting documentation, see my "New Light on *Leaves of Grass:* Whitman's Annotated Copy of the 1860 (Third) Edition," *Bulletin of the New York Public Library,* 69 (May 1965), 286n.

[3] And only one, "The City Dead-House," was of consequence.

during those "real parturition years," as he called them, must begin with an examination of the *Blue Book,* for it was during the war years that he reflected in his revisions the doubts, the sense of urgency, the despair, and, ultimately, the hope for the future of the Union he had experienced during this time.

A number of Whitman's revisions were not retained in the 1867 edition, and through a detailed study of all his revisions in the *Blue Book* we have an opportunity to observe the development of his ideas during this significant period of his career. From such a study we can gain a fresh insight into the published work by our ability to read the poems through their various stages of growth. In this paper I will briefly try to suggest the main, overall direction that his revisions took in the *Blue Book.*[4]

In the face of national disunity Whitman sought to impose on a number of the poems in the *Blue Book* a unity, a sense of order. Uppermost in his mind was a need for an organic oneness of all the States and of all Americans, coming together on terms of perfect equality. In the *Blue Book,* through the many revisions and excisions of poems in the 1860 text, the interlineations, erasures, restorations by erasure, paste-overs, holographs, marginal notes, the shifting of lines and stanzas from one section of a poem to another, all done variously in pencil, ink, blue pencil, and red pencil, emerges a single controlling idea out of which his imagery could proliferate, the dominating theme of nationalism, of the organic oneness of all the States and of their peoples, *South as well as North.*

His almost compulsive desire to achieve this poetic oneness served him well. The central theme of nationalism enabled him effectively to tie together the diverse though related experiences he wished to explore in depth in the 1860 text. However, before Whitman could establish this theme in his poetry, he obviously had to accept the South on equal terms with the rest of the country. Yet at the same time he held the South responsible for attempting to destroy the very unity of the States he now wished to establish. Here Whitman was faced with an artistic problem of considerable magnitude. He could hardly make a meaningful revision in the *Blue Book* toward the total pattern of thematic unity he needed as an artist (and for the most part ultimately achieved) until he had satisfactorily resolved this dilemma. This

[4] For a more detailed study, see my Introduction, *Walt Whitman's Blue Book* II, pp. xiii–lxi.

he did by holding in suspension two separate and distinct attitudes toward the South. In his prose, he had nothing but contempt for the South as a symbol of the force that would destroy the unity of the States. Yet in the *Blue Book* he was able to objectify this contempt in artistic terms by making the South, significantly not mentioned by name, symbolic of any aggressor that would attack the Union and whose fate it was to become ". . . an offal rank, / This day [of victory] to the dunghill maggots spurn'd." For the "other" South, the South of the "people," he extended his hand in friendship and left intact in the *Blue Book* the many existing favorable references to it that had appeared in the first three editions of *Leaves* (the 1855, '56, and '60), as well as specifically inserting others that brought together all the sections of the country on an equal footing.

It should be made clear that Whitman had not simply worked up an enthusiasm for the South during the war in order to accommodate his artistic needs. Quite the reverse was true. He had entertained few illusions regarding the North's moral posture before the war. He had consistently opposed slavery both on moral and economic grounds, arguing that white labor *"must not be degraded."* He was a free-soiler. He believed that the North, too, had played a strong part in advancing slavery. Fundamentally he held that the abolitionists' stand on slavery was excessive. He held a high opinion of Southerners generally, and, in fact, had ministered to wounded rebel as well as Federal soldiers in hospitals. He expressed deep sympathy for those Southern soldiers taken prisoner. All this contributed to his refusal to get caught up in the war hysteria current in the North, indulge in moral indignation, and condemn the South as the sole perpetrator of unspeakable villainies.

In the first three editions of *Leaves,* Whitman had skillfully developed in many of his poems what may be taken as his dominant metaphor, the "knit of identity," an image whose immediate sexual connotation reinforced his attempts to merge poetically America's physical greatness with the corresponding greatness of its people. Whitman was the self-proclaimed poet-prophet, the omnipresent "I" who transcended time and space in order to identify with those who, whatever their social class (his "divine average"),[5] contributed their share in making America a vital young nation. In the 1860 edition Whitman was able to support

---

[5] See *Walt Whitman's Blue Book* II, p. 418.

the structure of his poetic program with three special sections appearing here for the first time: "Chants Democratic," "Enfans d'Adam," and "Calamus."[6] In "Chants Democratic" he celebrated the greatness of America and its people; in Enfans d'Adam" and "Calamus" he provided a sexual basis for, respectively, the relationship between men and women ("amativeness") and the brotherhood and comradeship of man ("adhesiveness").[7]

Thus in the 1860 edition Whitman's poetic program had a thematic structure. With the coming of the Civil War, which in one stroke destroyed for the time the nationalistic base of his program, this structure collapsed. In the *Blue Book,* therefore, he attempted to impose a thematic order and unity on his poetry where none palpably existed in the real world around him. It had been precisely on this real world of an expanding and vigorous new nation that he had relied to justify his metaphor of an America whose physical greatness he equated with the greatness of its people. Whatever their social and political differences, they had at least not been at each other's throats.

Before the war Whitman had been able to counteract these differences with varying success in such typical poems as "Song of Myself," "The Sleepers," and "Crossing Brooklyn Ferry," to name but a few, by advancing a poetic program in which he declared that no such differences in his ideal world existed among the various social classes. This ideal of brotherhood (whether on the social or the sexual level) was crucial to him and he explored it as intensely in the *Blue Book* as he had before the war in the previous editions of *Leaves,* but with one significant difference: he demonstrated that so far as he was concerned the only way he could satisfactorily achieve the poetic unity, the organic oneness of the States he desired during this period, was to reject in his revisions any and all foreign influences on the embattled nation.

How far he was willing to carry his xenophobia may be mea-

---

[6] "Chants Democratic and Native American" was a group of twenty-one poems, sixteen of which appeared in the 1860 edition for the first time, and a prefatory poem, "Apostroph," which Whitman dropped in 1867. The poems in this group, which celebrate the theme of nationalism, were distributed in the 1867 edition and the group title was abandoned.

For titles initially found in the 1860 groupings and for the text of poems excluded from the final edition of *Leaves of Grass,* see Blodgett and Bradley, Bibliography, below ("Enfans d'Adam" was later titled "Children of Adam".)

[7] Whitman drew on phrenology for these descriptive terms. See Edward Hungerford, "Walt Whitman and His Chart of Bumps," *American Literature,* 2 (Jan. 1931), 350–384.

sured by what is perhaps Whitman's strongest expression of nationalism during this period, if not his entire career. At one point he added to the "Chants Democratic" poem "Our Old Feuillage" his wish to "demain [or cut America off from the rest of] the continent!" He probably realized he was carrying his nationalism too far and excised the line "Always our own feuillage! demain the continent!" in favor of the relatively mild "Always the compact union together of you and me and all!" (p. 159, line 3).

Actually, by stressing in the *Blue Book* an attitude of intense nationalism, Whitman was merely carrying to an excessive degree certain beliefs he had entertained as far back as 1842, when he was a twenty-two-year-old editor of the New York *Aurora.* He wanted America to stand on her own feet and shake off foreign influences, and he took pot-shots at those who "have so deplorable a passion for whatever is foreign." At the same time he denounced America's "slavish adoration" of things with "the stamp of foreign approbation," here specifically the "infallibility of London and Edinburgh critics." The *Aurora,* he said in a burst of patriotic fervor, "prides itself on being imbued with an *American* spirit!"

He continued the attack some years later in the Brooklyn *Eagle,* denouncing the flood of literary trash coming from abroad: "We have not enough confidence in our own judgments, . . ." he wrote, and "forget that God has given the American mind powers of analysis and acuteness superior to those possessed by any other nation on earth." And he assailed the old European orders of Russia, Austria, and Germany, speaking of the salutary effect of the "turbulence and destructiveness of the Democratic spirit" in those countries: "it is . . . from the Democracy, with its manly heart and its lion strength, spurning the ligatures wherewith drivellers would bind it—that we are to expect the great FUTURE of this Western World!" Consequently when England and France, among others, openly sided with the South, Whitman could hardly have been surprised. European countries—the old orders—were capable of any infamy.[8] Within this context, the intensity and at

---

[8] Whitman summed up his position in his note "Attitude of Foreign Governments During the War [1864]" (*The Collected Writings of Walt Whitman: Prose Works 1892, Specimen Days,* ed. Floyd Stovall, New York 1963, I, 93): ". . . There is certainly not one government in Europe but is now watching the war in this country, with the ardent prayer that the United States may be effectually split, crippled, and dismember'd by it. There is not one but would help toward that dismemberment, if it dared. I say such is the ardent wish to-day of England and of France, as governments, and of all the nations of Europe, as governments. . . . We are all too prone

times violence of Whitman's nationalism during the period of the war years become understandable.

However, in the Preface to the 1855 edition, Whitman had assumed his role of poet-prophet and idealized both the potentialities of the new nation and that which he had previously scorned, namely, the contributions of the past:

> America does not repel the past or what it has produced under its forms or amid other politics or the idea of castes or the old religions . . . . accepts the lesson with calmness. . . .

> The American poets are to enclose old and new for America is the race of races.

> Past and present and future are not disjoined but joined. The greatest poet forms the consistence of what is to be from what has been and is. He drags the dead out of their coffins and stands them again on their feet . . . . he says to the past, Rise and walk before me that I may realize you. He learns the lesson . . . . he places himself where the future becomes present.

In the light of Whitman's acceptance of the past and of foreign influences on America in the 1855 Preface, it is a curious irony that "By Blue Ontario's Shore," much of which he reworked from the Preface and which in 1860 was the lead patriotic poem of the "Chants Democratic" group, was heavily revised to become the most bitterly anti-foreign and intensely nationalistic of all the poems in the *Blue Book*.

The pliant structure of this seventeen-page poem (pp. 108–125) could easily accommodate Whitman's many revisions, insertions, deletions, and interlineations. In the 1860 version of the poem his reflections on the meaning of democracy easily proliferated out of his central metaphor, stated, characteristically, in the very first line: "A Nation announcing itself, (many in one,) . . ." What Whitman did here was to redefine this central metaphor in the light of his new Civil War experiences: by drawing on

---

to wander from ourselves, to affect Europe, and watch her frowns and smiles. *We need this hot lesson of general hatred* [my italics], and henceforth must never forget it. Never again will we trust the moral sense nor abstract friendliness of a single *government* of the old world."

He let stand without revision in the *Blue Book* his attack on the excesses of European aristocracy in "Song of the Broad-Axe," pp. 135–136, sts. 17–22. Similarly, "France, the 18th Year of These States," pp. 406–407 contains only a few minor revisions.

those experiences for his revisions he did not so much produce a new poem (he had retained a substantial portion of its 1860 text) as he indicated by strengthening the image of his persona, the Bard of Democracy, the poet-prophet, the conditions under which America's new unity would be achieved in the face of seeming disaster.

For these reasons his central metaphor had to be one that was definite yet at the same time elastic enough to accommodate the direction his other revisions were to take. That Whitman was aware of his problem is evidenced by his straining to establish the proper motif for his revision of "By Blue Ontario's Shore" (pp. 108–109), as through many complicated revisions he simultaneously held in mind both the 1860 version and the intended revised version of the poem.

He had initially inserted the following heavily revised trial lines in the bottom margin of p. 111:

> America, isolated, I sing, against all the remainder of the
>   earth,
> I say that works, songs, breathing the spirit of other lands
> Whether made here or imported, are so much poison to
>   These States[9]

He shifted the revised lines (with minor changes) to the beginning of the poem, taking the new title from the first line. He then revised the title to read, significantly, "*American* isolated, I sing," etc. (my italics). However, he was still not satisfied. He cancelled the title, indicating he would transfer these lines elsewhere in the poem.[10]

[9] Whitman (1863 notebook, *Walt Whitman and the Civil War,* ed. Charles I. Glicksberg, Philadelphia, 1933) had placed great stress on the fact that the "armies were composed mainly of American born & raised men. . . . We were all native born & made the main bulk of the soldiery." Glicksberg (144 N. 8) has observed that "Though Whitman acknowledged that there were Irish and German regiments who fought loyally and well, he stressed the point that the Union army was a native army; the Civil War was a national war." In a letter to his mother from Washington (15 April 1863, *Collected Writings of Walt Whitman: The Correspondence,* ed. Edwin H. Miller, New York, 1961, I, 88), Whitman wrote "it's a pity if we havn't Americans enough to put over our old war regiments—(I think less and less of foreigners, in this war—what I see, especially in the hospitals, convinces me that there is no other stock, for emergencies, but native American—no other name by which we can be saved)." Also see, e.g., *Correspondence,* I, 122, 134, and 148 for sentiments of a similar nature.

[10] He does not indicate where, but in *Songs Before Parting* (added as an annex to the 1867 edition) they appear on p. 5, sts. 11.1–2 and were dropped in 1881.

The new title and opening lines that he finally decided on (and retained in this position with minor changes in *Songs Before Parting*) were again taken from a revision he had made elsewhere in the poem. He added a title to a seven-line holograph he had pasted over stanzas 2–6 (p. 109), presumably to form a new stanza, and shifted them to the beginning of the poem:

> As I wandered the prairies alone at night
>
> As I wandered the Prairies alone at night,
> (As I mused of these mighty days & of peace returned, and the
>   dead that return no more,)
> A Phantom, gigantic, superb, with stern visage, arrested me,
> *Chant me a poem,* it said, *that breathes my native air alone,*
> 5   Chant me a song of *the throes of Democracy.*
>
> (Democracy, the destined conqueror—yet treacherous lip-
>   smiles every where,
> And death and infidelity at every step. . . .

This seven-line opening stanza was clearly better suited to Whitman's artistic needs than the severely restrictive opening trial lines he had rejected, since it permitted him to explore a wider range of experiences. While both openings stressed an intense nationalism, the second (in lines 5–7) permitted him to meditate not only on the meaning and the ultimate triumph of democracy but also (and without losing faith) on those negative forces at work to destroy the harmony and the unity of the ideal democratic society he was apotheosizing.[11]

[11] During an earlier revision he had inserted two trial lines (covered by the paste-over) between sts. 2–3. These lines exemplified in part what he was to mean by "the *throes of Democracy*" and by "treacherous lip-smiles every where, / And death and infidelity at every step": "(If we are lost O mother, O sisters dear no victor else has destroy'd us, / It is by ourselves we go down to eternal night)." However, he had balanced these lines with the affirmative

> We stand self-poised in the centre branching thence over the
>   world
> From Missouri, Nebraska, or Kansas, laughing attacks to
>   scorn. . . .

Cf. Whitman's revision of "Great Are the Myths," p. 200, 2.2 and 4.1. In 1860, 2.2–3 read "Helmsmen of nations, choose your craft! where you sail, I sail, / Yours is the muscle of life or death—yours is the perfect science—in you I have absolute faith." The trial line "I weather it out with you, or sink with you" replaced the cancelled (entire) "Yours is the muscle," etc. And to 4.1, "Great are the plunges, throes, triumphs, downfalls of Democracy," he added "(have you thought it would not rise again? have you thought it was not provided for in the essence of things?)"

Handwritten draft (Whitman's revisions):

As I wander'd the Prairies alone
at night,
A Phantom, gigantic, superb,
with stern visage, arrested me,
Chant me a poem, it said, that
breathes my native air alone,
Chant me a song of the throes of Democracy;

(Democracy, the destined conqueror—
yet treacherous lip-smiles everywhere,
And death and infidelity at every step,)

Printed text:

6. Produce great persons, the rest follows.

7. How dare a ~~sick man, or~~ an obedient ~~man,~~ write
   poems for The**r** States?
   Which is the theory or book that, for ~~our~~ purposes, is
   not diseased?

8. Piety and conformity to them that like!
   Peace, obesity, allegiance, to them that like!

10

A manuscript page showing part of Whitman's heavy revisions (in ink and pencil) for the opening stanza of the nationalistic poem "By Blue Ontario's Shore," in *Walt Whitman's Blue Book,* I (New York: The New York Public Library, 1968), p. 109. Reprinted by permission of The New York Library, Rare Book Division (Oscar Lion Collection).

Thus if in the 1860 version of the poem Whitman elsewhere confined himself to local areas: "I am he who goes through the streets with a barbed tongue, questioning every one I meet— questioning you up there now," in the *Blue Book* he responded to the demands of his nationalism by transcending such limitations to encounter the people of the entire nation: "I am he who walks the States with a barbed tongue, questioning every one I meet" (p. 110, 9.1).[12] He reinforced this declaration with the trial lines

> (With pangs & cries as your own O bearer of many children,
> This chant all wild to a race of pride I give. . . . (p. 110)

Similarly, "Are you, or would you be, better than all that has ever been before?" was revised to read, "O lands! would you be greater & freer than all that has been before?" And "If you would be better than all that has ever been before, come listen to me, and not otherwise" became "If you would be greater & freer than all that has been before, come listen to me" (p. 110, 10.1–2).

In 1860 Whitman announced that "Mighty bards have done their work, and passed to other spheres," but in the *Blue Book* he specifically rejected the heritage of the past by revising this line to read, "The poets of Asia and Europe have done their work, and passed to other spheres" (p. 110, 13.1).

Lines 5–7 of the revised opening stanza justify the seemingly abrupt shift in tone that occurs roughly midway through the revision of the poem. Strengthening the relatively mild 1860 line "Slavery, the tremulous spreading of hands to shelter it— the stern opposition to it, which ceases only when it ceases" to the angrier "Slavery, the murderous, treacherous conspiracy to raise it upon the ruins of all the rest" (p. 114, 17.40),[13] he added the trial line

> On & on to the grapple with it, (you over the Scorning
> assassin! then your life or ours be the stake—& respite
> no more. (p. 114)

The revision and trial line paved the way for the twelve-line

---

[12] Cf. "Our Old Feuillage," p. 165, line 77: "And I too of the Mannahatta, singing thereof—and no less in myself than the whole of the Mannahatta in itself," was revised to read, "And I too of the Mannahatta, singing thereof—singing the sights & songs of all my lands."

[13] The pasted sheet covered the words following "ruins of"; "all the rest," which completes the line, is taken from the published version in *Songs Before Parting*.

stanza he inserted immediately following them, which served as a counterpoint to the optimism he for the most part generated elsewhere in the poem. Here his attack on the South, unidentified by name, becomes in more general terms (and within the context of his total revisions of the poem) a pointed warning to *any* aggressor entertaining similar ambitions:

> Lo! High toward heaven, this day,
> Libertad! from the Conqueress' field return'd,
> I mark the new aureola around your head,
> No more of soft astral—but dazzling & fierce,
> 5 With war's flames, & the lambent lightnings playing;
> And your port immovable where you stand;
> With still the inextinguishable glance, & the clench'd
>   & lifted fist;
> And your foot on the neck of the one, the last great Scorner,
>   utterly crush'd beneath you;
> The menacing, arrogant one, that strode & advanced with his
>   senseless scorn, bearing the murderous knife;
> 10 Lo! the wide swelling one, the braggart, that would yesterday
>   do so much!
>   despised
> Already a carrion dead, & damned of all the earth—an offal
>   rank,
> This day to the dunghill maggots spurn'd.[14]

But if affirmation was quick in coming—to "O days of the future, I believe in you!" he added "I isolate myself for your sake!" (p. 114, 18.4), and "I lead the present with friendly hand toward the future" (p. 115, 18.7) was not revised—Whitman nevertheless viewed the immediate post-war situation with startling clarity in the trial lines

> (Soul of love & tongue of fire!
> Eyes to pierce the deepest deeps, & sweep the world!
> Mother prolific & teeming of all besides—yet barren, barren!)
> (p.115)

[14] In line 11 "damned" and "despised" were alternates. The holograph was written on the verso of the sheet containing the final eleven lines of the *Drum-Taps* (publ. May 1865) poem "Come Up from the Fields Father," indicating it was inserted after the war was over (an examination of the holograph, of course, also supports this view). Following the end of the war Whitman apparently had not mellowed in his attitude toward the South, but at least he was able to control his anger enough to objectify his contempt in artistic terms.

On the final page of the poem, Whitman inserted two three-line stanzas that affirmed in a quiet, reflective manner his belief in. the ultimate triumph of democracy:

> (Democracy! while weapons were every where aim'd at your
> breast,
> I saw you serenely give birth to children, saw in dreams your
> dilating form,
> Saw you with spreading mantle covering the world.)

> (Mother! bend down bend close to me your face!
> I know not what these plots & deferments are for,
> I know not success — but I know that your work goes on &
> must yet go on.) (p. 125)

Despite Whitman's many involved revisions for "By Blue Ontario's Shore," he felt the poem still needed more work (although basically the published poem followed its revised version) and he added the notation "take out & finish for future volume."[15]

In the *Blue Book* Whitman shows no let-up in his antagonism toward Europe and the traditions of the past, but in the 1867 edition he does indicate that he had undergone a significant, if isolated, change of heart. In "Starting from Paumanok," he had revised the line "See, the many-cylinder'd steam printing-press — See, the electric telegraph — See, the strong and quick locomotive, as it departs, panting, blowing the steam-whistle;" (p. 21, 63.8) to read as two lines: "See, the many-cylinder'd steam printing-press — See, the electric telegraph stretching across the continent, from the Western Sea to Manhattan, / See, the strong and quick," etc. In the 1867 edition (though not in the *Blue Book*) he inserted between them the separate line "See, through Atlantica's depths, pulses American, Europe reaching — pulses of Europe, duly return'd."

[15] In this connection, Whitman further strengthened the thematic unity of this poem when it appeared in *Songs Before Parting* by developing the theme of the "idea of perfect and free individuals," which he had passed over in the *Blue Book* with a few minor revisions. "Of the idea of perfect and free individuals, the idea of These States, the bard'walks in advance, leader of leaders," was revised in the *Blue Book* to read, "Of the idea of perfect and free individuals, / Of that idea the bard of These States walks in advance, leader of leaders," (p. 116, 24.1). In the published version this became "For the great Idea, the idea of perfect and free individuals, / For that idea, the bard walks in advance, leader of leaders. . . ." He fully developed this "great Idea" theme in the published version, strengthening the poem by adding to it five additional stanzas comprising twenty-one lines.

A year and a half had passed since Appomattox. Perhaps reflecting on the circumstance that the danger to the solidarity of the Union was now a thing of the past, Whitman had decided to make this gesture toward a reconciliation with Europe in order to mitigate somewhat the forceful and at times violent anti-foreign attitude he had exhibited in the *Blue Book, Drum-Taps,* and *Songs Before Parting* (all of whose poems came from the *Blue Book*). It is significant that thereafter he moved away from his preoccupation with the theme of nationalism to the theme of internationalism and the cosmic in such poems as "Passage to India" and "A Noiseless Patient Spider."[16]

II

Enfans d'Adam and Calamus

The lines that Whitman added in the *Blue Book* to the "Calamus" poem "Sometimes with One I Love"

> (I loved a certain person ardently, and my love was not re-
>   turned,
> But out of it I have written these songs.) (p. 376)

could easily have been written during the spring of 1859, when, as Fredson Bowers demonstrates in *Whitman's Manuscripts: Leaves of Grass (1860),* he "very likely" made fair copies of a "cluster"—or grouping—of twelve "Calamus—Leaves" poems in his private notebook.[17] Bowers conjectures that these twelve poems "appear to be highly unified and to make up an artistically

---

[16] In this connection, Whitman had revised the first line of the "Chants Democratic" poem "On Journeys through the States" from "Now we start hence, I with the rest, on our journeys through The States," to "On journeys through the States we start." However, after dropping the poem in 1867, he reprinted it in *Passage to India* (1871), where he had added the following lines, giving to the poem the international motif it lacked in 1860 and in the *Blue Book* revision:

> On journeys through the States we start,
> (Ay through the world, urged by these songs,
> Sailing henceforth to every land, to every sea,).

[17] (Chicago 1955), p. lxxi.

complete story of attachment, crisis, and renunciation."[18] From some past, negative experience Whitman extracted what was to serve as his indispensable metaphor of intense attachment, loneliness, and despair in the "Calamus-Leaves" cluster and in most of the poems in the 1860 "Calamus" group as well.

Apparently Whitman had had the inner strength to resolve the personal crisis that impelled him to publish these morbid confessions. He was perhaps more fortunate than others of the same temperament because he had found available to him in this crucial period of his life two significant emotional safety valves through which he was able to relieve the tension and strain that arose from his homosexual sensibility: through his poetry he was able to convey in the most direct manner possible the torments that issued from his dilemma of being "different" from other men (which he stressed in the "Calamus" poems "Whoever You are Holding Me Now in Hand" and "Are You the New Person Drawn toward Me?"), and he was able to sublimate this emotion in a poetic program having as its basis the brotherhood of man. During the war volunteers were needed to care for the needs of the wounded soldiers, and Whitman was able to perform this patriotic service in hospitals in New York and Washington.

The personal crisis in Whitman's life that led him to create the "Calamus-Leaves" cluster and the "Calamus" poems may have been resolved, at least outwardly, by the time the 1860 edition was published.[19] However, given the intensity of his expression of this personal dilemma in the "Calamus" poems, it seems reasonable to conclude that the nature of his activities during the war,

---

[18] Page lxvi. The twelve poems, Bowers relates, were part of a larger group he had composed and numbered earlier with the intention of including them in the forthcoming 1860 edition (p. lxiii). Initially the theme of "adhesiveness" was treated in a general way—the dominant symbol was "Live Oak with Moss," which he later changed to the stronger and more suggestive "Calamus-Leaves" (p. lxxii). He grouped and numbered these poems ("I–XII") in his notebook and in the 1860 edition distributed them among the forty-five "Calamus" poems appearing here for the first time. Nos. I–XII (with revisions) correspond to the following "Calamus" poems (p. lxiv): I—"Not Heat Flames Up and Consumes"; II—"I Saw in Louisiana a Live-Oak Growing"; III—"When I Heard at the Close of the Day"; IV—"This Moment Yearning and Thoughtful"; V—"Long I Thought that Knowledge"—dropped in 1867; VI—"What Think You I Take My Pen in Hand?"; VII—"Recorders Ages Hence"; VIII—"Hours Continuing Long"—dropped in 1867; IX—"I Dream'd in a Dream"; X—"O You Whom I Often and Silent Come"; XI—"Earth, My Likeness"; XII—"To a Western Boy."

[19] Not all the 1860 "Calamus" poems celebrated the theme of "adhesiveness": e.g., "That Music Always Round Me," "What Place is Besieged?" and "What Ship Puzzled at Sea."

in which he came into such close contact with the soldiers, had reinvoked within him this strong emotion.

It is not surprising, therefore, that while Whitman's revisions for the "Enfans d'Adam" group were relatively light (except for "A Woman Waits for Me"), he exhibited a great deal more critical concern for his revisions of the "Calamus" poems. Although he did not reject any of the "Enfans d'Adam" poems in the *Blue Book,* he saw fit to drop "In the New Garden" in 1867, doubtless for artistic reasons. Despite its inclusion in the 1860 "Enfans d'Adam" group, "In the New Garden" celebrated the theme of "amativeness" only in the most general way.

However, while he also rejected in the *Blue Book* the three "Calamus" poems he later dropped in the 1867 edition,[20] he had initially rejected no fewer than thirteen "Calamus" poems,[21] four of which, "Recorders Ages Hence," "A Glimpse," "A Promise to California," and "To a Western Boy," he restored. Thus if he had followed through on his final *Blue Book* revisions for this group, nine "Calamus" poems (or one-fifth of the group) would have disappeared. At first glance it might appear that he had gone through the forty-five-poem "Calamus" section with the idea of eliminating highly personal and revealing statements on the theme of "adhesiveness." Had Whitman intended to suppress passages or entire poems that delineated his homosexual sensibility, he certainly would have done so in the extensively revised "Calamus" group. Any logical assumption of suppression would immediately presuppose the outright elimination or the watering down of poems, stanzas, lines. On the contrary, in poem after poem Whitman retained through extensive revision passages as revealing as anything he rejected. Within the context of his total revisions for this group, the evidence is clear that he had rejected the nine poems for artistic reasons, in order to avoid repeating the same theme and emotion he had explored variously throughout "Calamus" in the 1860 edition.[22]

[20] "Long I Thought that Knowledge," "Hours Continuing Long," and "Who is Now Reading This?"

[21] The three in note 20 and "Recorders Ages Hence," "Are you the New Person Drawn toward Me?" "I Hear it was Charged against Me," "A Glimpse," "A Promise to California," "What Think You I Take My Pen in Hand?," "A Leaf for Hand in Hand," "Fast-Anchor'd Eternal O Love," "Here the Frailest Leaves of Me," and "To a Western Boy."

[22] In another connection, James E. Miller, Jr., *A Critical Guide to Leaves of Grass* (Chicago, 1957) pp. 52–79, compares the "Calamus" poems in the 1860 edition with those in the final (1892) edition of *Leaves* and concludes that the latter "certainly do not reveal a pattern of suppression or concealment. In almost every in-

Enfans d'Adam

With the exception of "A Woman Waits for Me," Whitman appears to have been satisfied with his expression of "amativeness" in this group of fifteen poems. He had initially marked "A Woman Waits for Me" "satisfactory Jan '65" (the title page of the "Enfans d'Adam" group bears the notation "All satisfactory—Jan '65") but later amended the "Jan" to "July" after making further revisions in the poem. "A Woman Waits for Me" was extensively revised from a poem whose dominant metaphor was one of "amativeness" to one whose imagery supported the burden of Whitman's nationalism during this period. Significantly, "A Woman Waits for Me" became in revision *"A Woman America knows."* However, at some point between July 1865 and September 1866 (when the 1867 edition was in the press), Whitman rejected *"A Woman America knows"* in favor of the 1860 version, retaining it with minor changes in the 1867 "Children of Adam" group.[23]

In "To the Garden the World" he added only a trial title taken, characteristically, from the first line and a word which he brought in from the margin and erased. Five poems, "Native Moments," "Once I Pass'd through a Populous City," "O Hymen! O Hymenee!" "I am He that Aches with Love," "As Adam Early in the Morning," contain forthright and explicit expressions of the theme of "amativeness" and show light revisions in which he added trial titles, altered terminal punctuation, tightened a line by replacing a word or substituting one word for another, and the like.

Similarly, "From Pent-up Aching Rivers," "I Sing the Body Electric," "Spontaneous Me," "One Hour to Madness and Joy," "We Two, How Long We were Fool'd," and "Ages and Ages Returning at Intervals," several of which are lengthy poems, contain moderate revisions in which he cancelled several lines, added

---

stance, sufficient artistic reasons can be found to justify the change [i.e., the dropping of three 'Calamus' poems, the transfer of four to other sections of *Leaves,* and the adding of a poem] undertaken. By and large, the 'Calamus' section remained in essence the same through some thirty years of revision" (p. 63).

[23] He probably decided to stay with the 1860 version for the same reason that impelled him, following the end of the war, to insert the line in the 1867 text but not in the *Blue Book* in which he reached toward a reconciliation with Europe and the traditions of the past after having made so many revisions which were motivated by his nationalism. What is clear, however, is that he did not alter the poem in this manner because he may have panicked after his dismissal by Harlan on 30 June. We have already seen that Whitman had allowed the bulk of the lines containing explicit references to sex to stand throughout the *Blue Book.*

short phrases, and changed terminal punctuation but did not alter the tone of the poems or delete the explicit references to sex he had included in the 1860 edition.

Of the remaining two, "Facing West from California's Shores" and "In the New Garden," he inserted a trial line in "Facing West" and tightened the poem by deletion and replacement. In "In the New Garden," in which he reflects on the meaning of death, he did the same by cancelling four of the nine lines and replacing one of the cancelled lines with a trial line. His revisions of the "Enfans d'Adam" poems were, except for "A Woman Waits for Me," light to moderate, and the most explicit sexual passages in such poems as "From Pent-up Aching Rivers," "I Sing the Body Electric," "Spontaneous Me," and "One Hour to Madness and Joy" were allowed to stand.[24]

Calamus

It would be difficult to assign as the reason for Whitman's initial rejection of thirteen and restoration of four "Calamus" poems in the *Blue Book* solely his desire to eliminate highly personal and revealing statements on the theme of "adhesiveness." While the three "Calamus" poems he dropped in 1867 clearly reflect the loneliness and despair that resulted from his inability to maintain such a relationship, many of the "Calamus" poems that he retained in the *Blue Book* were equally revealing, especially the heavily revised "Whoever You are Holding Me Now in Hand," in which he explores the theme of "adhesiveness" with almost a compulsive intensity.

"Whoever You Are" was revised in three separate stages. To the revised stanzas 4–7, Whitman added the trial title *"By stealth in some wood O my lover,"* and this constituted the final version of the poem in the *Blue Book*. "O my lover," which he added in the final stage of revision to the end of several lines, became a motif which reinforced the personal, secretive tone of

---

[24] For example, Whitman's only deletion in "Spontaneous Me" occurred in line 10 (this line was retained in 1867) and clearly was made for artistic reasons: "This poem [i.e., the male sex organ] drooping shy and unseen, that I always carry, and that all men carry. . . ." However, in 1860 he had repeated the same idea in line 11: "(Know, once for all, avowed on purpose, wherever are men like me, are our lusty, lurking, masculine, poems,) . . ." With the exception of line 10, the explicit references in this poem to the sex act and to the organs of the body were all retained in the *Blue Book* save for changes in terminal punctuation, etc.

stanzas 4-7. And he retained intact in the *Blue Book* many of the 1860 lines of "Whoever You Are."

He revised his initial trial title *"By stealth in a wood for trial"* to the more evocative *"By stealth in some wood O my lover."* The following is a fair copy of Whitman's revisions for the third and final stage of "Whoever You Are."[25]

[By stealth in some wood O my lover]

[[4. Or else, only]] [B]y stealth, in some wood, [[for trial,]]
        [O my lover] or back of a rock, in the open air [[,]]
    (For in any roofed room of a house I emerge not—nor in
            company,
    And in libraries I lie as one dumb, a gawk, or unborn,
            or dead,)
    But just possibly [specially] with you on a high hill [[—first]]
    [W]atching lest any person, for miles around, approach
            unawares,
    Or possibly with you sailing at sea, or on the beach of the sea,
            or some quiet island,
    Here to put your lips upon mine I permit you,
    With the comrade's long-dwelling kiss, or the new husband's
            kiss,
    For I am the new husband, and I am the comrade.
    [But I am not what you supposed, O my lover.]

  5. Or, if [[you will,]]* thrusting me beneath your clothing,
    Where I may [[feel the throbs of your heart, or]]* rest [[upon
            your]] [on your waist or] hip,
    Carry me when you go forth over land or sea;
    For thus, merely touching you, is enough—is [[best,]] [better
            for both of us,]
    And thus, touching you, would I silently sleep and be carried
            eternally.
    [On your breast, on your silent breast O my lover]

  6. But these leaves [opening you open] [[conning, you con]]
            at peril,
    For these leaves, and me, you will not understand, [O my
            lover,]
    They will elude you at first, and still more afterward—I will
            certainly elude you,

---

[25] Retained insertions in Whitman's hand are bracketed. All cancelled portions of the text are double-bracketed and cancellations restored by erasure are double-bracketed and starred. All are final readings.

Even while you should think you had unquestionably caught
    me, behold!
Already you see I have escaped from you[[.]] [, O my lover,]
[Therefore set me down of your own accord
Release your hands from my shoulders & let me go.]

7. For it is not for what I have put into it that I have written
    this book,
    Nor is it by reading it you will acquire it, [O my lover,]
    Nor do those know me best who admire me[[,]] and vauntingly
        praise me,
    [[Nor will the candidates for my love, (unless at most a very
        few,) prove victorious,]]
    Nor will my poems do good only—they will do just as much
        evil, perhaps more[[,]][[;]]
    [[For all is useless without that which you may guess at
        many times and not hit—that which I hinted at,]]
    Therefore release me, [at once, take off your hands from my
        shoulders]
    [Put me down] and depart on your way [[.]] [O my lover.]

Similarly, Whitman strengthened and personalized the theme
of "adhesiveness" in the four-line "To a Western Boy." He inter-
lined "O boy of the west! to you O my loving boy!" above (and
replacing) the printed line 1 and revised lines 1–4 (now 2–5), as
follows: "To the young man, many things to absorb, to engraft,
to develop, I teach, to help him become élève of mine" became
"To you many things I teach, to help you become élève of mine";
"But if blood like mine circle not in your veins" became "For
all that if blood like mine circle not in your veins"; "you" replaced
"he," to read, "If you be not silently selected by lovers, and do not
silently select lovers"; and "Of what use is it that he seek to become élève of mine?" became "Of what use were it to become
élève of mine?"
    He retained without revision the most revealing lines in
"When I Heard at the Close of the Day," in which he describes
the joys he experienced when he and the one he loves "most"
"lay sleeping . . . under the same cover in the cool night":

6 And when I thought how my dear friend, my lover, was on
    his way coming, O then I was happy;
. . . .
8 And the next [day] came with equal joy—And with the next,
    at evening, came my friend;

And that night, while all was still, I heard the waters roll
    slowly continually up the shores,
10 I heard the hissing rustle of the liquid and sands, as directed
    to me,[26] whispering, to congratulate me,
For the one I love most lay sleeping by me under the same
    cover in the cool night,
— In the stillness, in the autumn moonbeams, his face was
    inclined toward me,
And his arm lay lightly around my breast — And that night I
    was happy.

In the revealing "I Saw in Louisiana a Live-Oak Growing,"
"To a Stranger," and "That Shadow My Likeness" he inserted
trial titles but made no revisions in the text. In "Earth My Likeness" he added a trial title and corrected only a letter that in
1860 had been set in the wrong font. These lines stood unrevised:

I now suspect there is something fierce in you, eligible to
    burst forth;
5   For an athlete is enamoured of me — and I of him,
But toward him there is something fierce and terrible in me,
    eligible to burst forth,
I dare not tell it in words — not even in these songs.

Fourteen of the "Calamus" poems are personally revealing
in various degrees and contain only light revisions.[27] Similarly he
retained eleven poems with moderate revisions and (with an occa-
sional minor exception) variously let stand the sexual imagery or

---

[26] "as directed to me," was cancelled. In line 12 a dash was inserted preceding
"In."

[27] "Scented Herbage of My Breast," "Not Heaving from my Ribb'd Breast
Only," "Roots and Leaves Themselves Alone," "Not Heat Flames up and Con-
sumes," "Trickle Drops," "Of Him I Love Day and Night," "City of Orgies," "That
Music Always Round Me," "This Moment Yearning and Thoughtful," "We Two
Boys Together Clinging," "O Living Always, Always Dying," "What Place is Besieged?" and "What Ship Puzzled at Sea," "To the East and to the West," and
"Full of Life Now."
He cancelled the notation "? Calamus. ?to lead the separate vol?" inserted next
to "Scented Herbage," the second poem in the "Calamus" group. It is difficult to
tell by this ambiguous notation whether at one point he intended "Scented Herbage" to lead "the separate vol," i.e., of the next (1867) edition; or of only "Calamus"
poems; or whether the entire "Calamus" group except the opening poem, "In Paths
Untrodden," would lead the next edition. In all events in 1867 "Scented Herbage"
follows "In Paths Untrodden" and the "Calamus" group follows "Children of Adam"
with the poem "Excelsior" separating them.

strengthened it. And he made changes for artistic reasons by tightening or excising a line, and the like.[28]

Of the four poems he rejected and restored, "Recorders Ages Hence," "A Glimpse," "To a Western Boy," and "A Promise to California," the first three are certainly as revealing as any he rejected, and whatever changes he made in no way altered their sharply delineated theme of "adhesiveness." It would appear then that his rejection of the nine "Calamus" poems (of which "Are You the New Person Drawn toward Me?" was marked "Out without fail" and "A Leaf for Hand in Hand" was not revealing by anybody's standards) must be attributed to reasons other than that they betrayed the expression of highly personal emotions he wished to obliterate in the 1867 edition.

Let us examine the three he dropped from *Leaves of Grass* in 1867, "Long I Thought that Knowledge," "Hours Continuing Long,"[29] and "Who is Now Reading This?"

In "Long I Thought that Knowledge" the poet declares that

10   I heed knowledge, and the grandeur of The States, and the
     example of heroes, no more,
   I am indifferent to my own songs—I will go with him I love,
   It is to be enough for us that we are together—We never
     separate again.

We have seen that Whitman's nationalism during this period ran counter to this sentiment. He doubtless rejected "Long I Thought" for this reason and not because it was any more revealing than the others. Further, the poem was rejected without a single revision or even the inclusion of a trial title.

The plaintive lines 1–4 of "Hours Continuing Long" contain light revisions, with only "of the dusk" cancelled in line 2: "Hours of the dusk, when I withdraw to a lonesome and unfrequented spot, seating myself, leaning my face in my hands." He revised

[28] "In Paths Untrodden," "These I Singing in Spring," "Of the Terrible Doubt of Appearances," "When I Heard at the Close of the Day," "Behold This Swarthy Face," "The Prairie-Grass Dividing," "When I Peruse the Conquer'd Fame," "No Labor-Saving Machine," "I Dream'd in a Dream," "Sometimes with One I Love," and "Among the multitude."

[29] At some point Whitman had doubts about rejecting "Long I Thought" and "Hours Continuing Long"; next to the former he wrote the notation "Out" preceded by a question mark and drew cancelling lines through the text; next to the latter he wrote "Out for revision" and "Out," after revising the poem at least to lines 8 or 9, but drew no cancelling lines through the text.

lines 5: "Hours when I am forgotten, (O weeks and months are passing, but I believe I am never to forget!)" and 6: "Sullen and suffering hours! (I am ashamed—but it is useless—I am what I am;)" to read as the new line 5: "—Hours when I am forgotten, sullen and suffering hours!" After making several revisions in which he tightened lines 7 and 8, he joined them, to read:

7 Hours of my torment—is there over the whole earth one other
    man like me
8 Is he as I am now distracted—his friend, his lover, lost to him?

He revised line 9, "Is he too as I am now? Does he still rise in the morning, dejected, thinking who is lost to him? and at night, awaking, think who is lost?" to read: "Does he rise in the morning, dejected, thinking who is lost to him? or at night, awaking, think who is lost?" The introspective and revealing lines 10–12 show no revisions:

10 Does he too harbor his friendship silent and endless? harbor
    his anguish and passion?
Does some stray reminder, or the casual mention of a name,
    bring the fit back upon him, taciturn and deprest?
Does he see himself reflected in me? In these hours, does he
    see the face of his hours reflected?

While Whitman's (unrevised) confession of guilt in "Who is Now Reading This?" for "the stuff of wrong-doing"—". . . (O conscience-struck! O self-convicted!) / . . . as if I do not secretly love strangers! . . ."—was certainly highly personal and revealing, it is difficult to see where it is more revealing than, say, the final revision of "Whoever You are Holding Me Now in Hand," the lightly revised "Earth, My Likeness," or for that matter any of the other poems in the "Calamus" group which he retained with light or moderate revisions.

By October 1866, *Leaves of Grass* with three annexes—*Drum-Taps, Sequel to Drum-Taps,* and *Songs Before Parting*—was in print, and Whitman expressed to his mother his relief that the difficult job of getting the book out was over:

. . . I feel satisfied with the looks of it—it might be better, & handsomer paper, &c—but I am glad it turns out as good as it is. . . . Then

I feel sure it tells the meaning better than any of the former editions—
My enemies, & those who are determined to find fault, will of course
still do so—But I feel that the book proves itself to any fair person—
& will have a fair chance now, & go ahead. But the best thing is, it is
done—& I shant worry myself any more with fixing & revising it.
(*Correspondence,* I, 288)

A comparison of the 1860 and 1867 editions indicates in the
clearest possible manner the extent of Whitman's enormous creative activity during the war years. And an examination of the *Blue
Book,* whose heavily and painstakingly revised 1860 text served as
the basis for the 1867 edition, makes it possible for us to understand why and how he responded as he did in his poetry to the
pressures of war. On the evidence his optimism over the 1867 edition was justified.

Part IV   Democratic Vistas

Richard Chase

"The Theory of America"

Like all of Whitman's prophetic utterances, *Democratic Vistas* (1871) is a transcendental version of Jeffersonian-Jacksonian democracy, the credo which Whitman had more literally expressed in his earlier newspaper writings, particularly the editorials in the Brooklyn *Eagle* and *Times*. The idea of progress becomes the principle of the universe—as we look up from our provisional Pisgah we behold the orbic forms of a benevolent, self-purifying cosmos; as we lower our gaze the vistas out over the continent darken somewhat and are populated with villages, rivers, fields of wheat, factories, mechanics, farmers, patient mothers, small property holders, town meetings—a notably if evanescently envisioned myth of social life.

The absence in *Democratic Vistas* of direct political recommendation may be traced to Whitman's lifelong distrust of government. It may also be traced to Whitman's disillusion with practical politics, which he had long since given up in disgust, saying, for example, that the presidents immediately preceding Lincoln had all been "deform'd, mediocre, snivelling, unreliable, false-hearted men." He had always believed that social reform was a matter of individual regeneration, was not a political but a moral and spiritual problem; and all the weakness and strength of this view are in *Democratic Vistas*. One may note, however, the passage where Whitman momentarily fears he has gone too far in rejecting politics and, even though "these savage, wolfish parties alarm me," urges young men to take up a political career.

The individualism Whitman always championed becomes in *Democratic Vistas* his doctrine for "personalism"; his lifelong belief in free trade is spiritualized into a vision of international amity. The moral-prophetic office of the poet on which the *Vistas* insists, had, of course, already been insisted on in the 1855 Preface. But although in many ways *Democratic Vistas* is a restatement of old views, Whitman's strong reaction to the spectacle of the Grant Administration and the Gilded Age gives the piece a novel emphasis on the need for "more compaction and more moral identity" in what the author took to be perilously anarchic times, and it also accounts for the intense concern with "personalism" and the unprecedented urgency with which the great function of the "literatus" is asserted.

Democratic Vistas shares some of that indistinctness of outline which many people now seem to find in nineteenth-century social polemic, overladen as it often was by merely ethical and prophetic tendencies. Doubtless we miss a certain hardheaded but humane pragmatism in listening to the exhortations of Whitman, as we miss also a genuine sense of history. True, Whitman is capable of historical or political realism. He echoes Mill, Arnold, and Tocqueville in saying that no one ought to "debate to-day whether to hold on, attempting to lean back and monarchize, or to look forward and democratize—but *how,* and in what degree or part, most prudently to democratize." This is a simple observation, but it is also a breath of fresh air in an atmosphere that is sometimes oppressively thick. Whitman can even write that "we do not (at least I do not) put it either on the ground that the People, the masses, even the best of them, are, in their latent or exhibited qualities, essentially sensible and good—nor on the ground of their rights; but that good or bad, rights or no rights, the democratic formula is the only safe and preservative one for coming times," and this is gratifyingly free of jargon.

Whitman can say, too, "I hail with joy the oceanic, variegated, intense practical energy, the demand for facts, even the business materialism of the current age, our States. But woe to the age or land in which these things, movements, stopping at themselves, do not tend to ideas." Matthew Arnold himself might almost have written this. And the *Vistas* is in fact much closer to the general run of nineteenth-century Anglo-Saxon social prophecy than it is to the French enlightenment, Hegel, or Marx. It is true that Whitman fancied himself as something of a Hegelian and even wrote to Edward Dowden that in *Democratic Vistas,* he meant to "project . . . an entirely new breed of authors, poets, American, comprehensive, Hegelian, Democratic, religious." But Whitman's second-

hand idea of Hegel is indistinguishable from the loose transcendentalist dialectic he had found in Emerson, and perhaps Carlyle, and
had "promulged" in "Song of Myself."

The truth is that *Democratic Vistas* is a kind of American
version of Arnold's *Culture and Anarchy,* despite the fact that
Whitman and Arnold were very little disposed to believe they had
anything in common and despite Whitman's attacks, in the *Vistas,*
on "culture" and "the grand style," both of which he understood
to be mere dilettantism. But do not both authors believe that the
present danger in their countries is anarchy, that modern man
places too great a faith in the mere machinery of legislation, that
lively, elevating ideas should be current, that the middle class is
the one to rely on, that aggressive assertions of material progress,
including the mass production of vulgar literature, may cloak a
virulent moral sickness, that poetry has a very broad function, including that of religion? In one important respect Whitman was
more "Arnoldian" than Arnold—to the extent, that is, that his
sense of things remained rather too exclusively ethical and literary
and lacked historical objectivity.

But *Democratic Vistas* is broadly American in spirit, not only
in its native idealism, its large hopefulness, its lack of concern
with the limitations of life, its disinclination to understand that
society is based on contradictions which may be humanly tragic
but that nevertheless "freedom," "personalism," "compaction and
moral identity" cannot be understood or exist outside of society.
Also characteristic of our native mind is the swinging back and
forth from minute realism to the most ultimate and ideal of con-
siderations. Whitman finds it perfectly natural on one page to im-
ply that democracy may turn out to be unworkable but that history
has stuck us with it and we must face the fact and, on another page,
to say that democracy should not be confined to the political
sphere but should be extended, like a redemptive spirit, to every
part of life including manners, religion, and literature, as well as
the Army and Navy. Again, Whitman can be exact and particular
in his denunciation of the social scene but the closest he gets to
describing what an admirable American society might be is his
pleasing but impalpable vision of "some pleasant western settlement or town, where a couple of hundred best men and women,
of ordinary worldly status, have by luck been drawn together."

The fundamental contradiction of *Democratic Vistas* is, of
course, one of which Whitman is intensely aware: "This idea of
perfect individualism it is indeed that deepest tinges and gives

character to the idea of the aggregate. For it is mainly or alto-gether to serve independent separation that we favor a strong generalization, consolidation." Just how the claims of the individual and those of the aggregate are to be harmoniously reconciled without destroying either is certainly a basic political question. More strongly than anywhere else in his writings, Whitman urges the importance of national unity. But like most Americans of his time Whitman, although capable of understanding unity as consisting in a commonalty of tradition and experience, could not understand that this felt unity must express itself in laws and institutions evolving in history, that it must be made practicable by the social intelligence. Doubtless the Grant Administration exhibited few enough of these unifying political forces. But Whitman's mind was incapable of supplying them. Instead he offered his old solution: the ideal of "perfect comradeship."

It would surely have outraged Whitman to have been told that *Democratic Vistas* shows less knowledge of political realities and a weaker sense of history than *Culture and Anarchy* (to take up again the comparison), or that insofar as he is political at all he is, in an important sense, more conservative than Arnold. Yet both these propositions are true. As for the relative conservatism of these two writers, we have only to ask what, in the *Vistas* and in *Culture and Anarchy,* is taken to be the central and determining fact about the societies to which they refer. The given fact in Arnold's book is historical change of the most portentous sort, for Arnold is as impressed as Tocqueville by the historic forward march of the democratization of the Western world. This change entails a radical departure from all past experience. Arnold's conservatism is confined to his attempt to modify the course of democratization in accordance with the traditional values he cherishes. But he is clearly committed to basic changes.

The given fact in *Democratic Vistas* is a set of American beliefs and attitudes—"the American programme"—which was "put on record" once and for all in "the compacts of the Declaration of Independence" and "the Federal Constitution." The business of poets is not to "criticize life" but to reveal the given "compacts," to furnish the "archetypes" of thought and experience implied by what providence has decreed America to be. From this point of view, Whitman will not even admit that historical change is possible. For despite all his appeals to the future greatness of America there is nothing in this future which is not merely a further revelation of the totally adequate dispensation vouchsafed to Americans at the birth of the Republic. Change is understood as a progressive discovery of something already given, though not at first correctly or clearly perceived in its entirety. If Arnold tends to think of England as hastening perilously into the problematical future, Whitman thinks of America as exploring her "exhaustless mines of the richest ore" and as furnishing out the future with that which has already been given—a future which cannot help being better than the present because it will be a fuller, a more valid realization of what providence decreed America to be in 1776, Whitman seems to think, when to all intents and purposes history stopped, its final purpose of outdating "feudalism" and announcing democracy having been accomplished. History is, as it were, a kind of great mother whose divine duty it was to bear a democratic son to succeed a tyrannical father. Thus the true prophet (says Whitman in *Specimen Days*) does not so much "predict" as "reveal and outpour" the "inner, divine spontaneities" of the soul. One of the paradoxes of Whitman's work is that prophecy as a wild, spontaneous poetic outflowing is the source both of the radical, utopian indeterminacy of "Song of Myself" and the fundamentally conservative political ideas of *Democratic Vistas*. And this paradox is, of course, not only Whitman's. Probably more often than not it is the function of prophecy itself to be emotionally and poetically wild, rhapsodic, and visionary while maintaining conservative political or religious views. At any rate, this paradox is native to the democratic mind. Most Americans, certainly most of our great writers past and present, can see themselves in one form or another in that "conservative Christian anarchist" Henry Adams declared himself to be.

Democratic Vistas is not the great piece of radical social ideology it has sometimes been called. Like most American social thinking, it is conservative, individualistic, and unhistorical. But if this native habit of mind, together with the author's too exclusive preoccupation with moral, spiritual, and literary values, weakened his grasp of political reality, his appraisal of the individual is acute and persuasive, and his account of literature as the force which must reconcile individual and aggregate, though absurd to the extent that it is taken as a direct political recommendation, has its relevance to social actualities.

That celebration of the "simple separate person" which Whitman had come to call "personalism" is the glory of *Democratic Vistas*. "Personalism" is merely Whitman's new word for "identity," but in *Democratic Vistas* the idea is insisted on with a new urgency and beheld with a new clarity. Whitman's greatness had always rested in his ability to describe the plight and career of the self in all of its "singleness and normal simplicity and separation," as he says in the *Vistas,* as well as in the astonishing and ever novel modes of its entanglement with the world in which it exists. In "Song of Myself" we have the comic dance of the self becoming alternately entangled in and extricated from the complicated web of human life and the universe. Here the self was conceived as a kind of coy, elusive, democratic Pan. In "Out of the Cradle" and "As I Ebb'd with the Ocean of Life" the poet had chanted his great dirges on the separation of the self, the plight and pathos of singleness. Here the self had been conceived psychologically and metaphysically. In *Democratic Vistas* the self is intuitively perceived as an irreducible fact of personal and social experience, not immediately as a *political* fact, but as a fact without which there can be no humane politics:

> There is, in sanest hours, a consciousness, a thought that rises independent, lifted out from all else, calm, like the stars, shining eternal. This is the thought of identity—yours for you, whoever you are, as mine for me. Miracle of miracles, beyond statement, most spiritual and vaguest of earth's dreams, yet hardest basic fact, and only entrance to all facts. In such devout hours, in the midst of the significant wonders of heaven and earth (significant only because of the Me in the center), creeds, conventions, fall away and become of no account before this simple idea. Under the luminousness of real vision, it alone takes possession, takes value. Like the shadowy dwarf in the fable, once liberated and look'd upon, it expands over the whole earth, and spreads to the roof of heaven.

It is hardly possible to imagine a more vital and necessary intuition than this. For surely one may judge whether or not a nation can be called civilized by the extent to which it is able to keep this "most spiritual and vaguest of earth's dreams, yet hardest basic fact" vitally operative. The conditions of the modern world are not conducive to sustaining in the mind "the quality of Being, in the object's self." Fewer and fewer people either have or know how to value Whitman's sense of how the sources of our being pour ever novel forms of vitality into the self and of how the self can be sustained in a hostile world.

Without at all discounting the incalculable value of Whitman's "personalism," one must nevertheless note that he characteristically tries to make it do too much. Not having anything like so clear an intuition of society or of history as he has of the self, he believes only in the self and asks it to do what society ought at least assist in doing. Thus "personalism" not only discovers and asserts the personal; it also, in some unspecified realm of being, "fuses" men into "solidarity."

This is where literature comes in. The "literatuses" of the future will create the kind of instinctive national mind necessary to the resolution of the contradictions of democracy, the purification of its evils, the toughening of its moral and physical being, and the final establishment of the comradely ideal. Whitman believes that so far America has no "real literature" and has produced no literatuses. Apparently not even Emerson is a literatus, not to mention Cooper, Hawthorne, Poe, Thoreau, and Melville. What kind of literature is it that Whitman finds at once not existent and desirable?

The coming American literature must have native roots—art forms "touch a man closest (perhaps only actually touch him) . . . in their expression through autochthonic lights and shades." American poetry must be "bold, modern, and all-surrounding and kosmical"; it must illustrate the people and respond to the slang, the folkways, the vast spectacle of the expanding country; it should not respond to the "covert, the lurid, the maleficent, the devil, the grim estimates inherited from the Puritans, hell, natural depravity, and the like"; it must be morally sound (not, of course, prudish) and appeal to the "absolute Conscience"; it must treat of nature in her universal, cosmical aspect and as the manifestation of the All; it must culminate in "metaphysics"—that is, in an inquiry into "the mysteries of the spiritual world, the soul itself, and the question of the immortal continuation of our identity"; finally it should possess "great poems of death."

In these prescriptions for American literature Whitman is very far from reality. Although his literary ideal corresponds to his own worst poems, it corresponds only partly to his best. Although it is a fair description of much of our second-rate literature, it has little relation to the first-rate either before Whitman or after. If American writing at its best was to be seen in such works as *Huckleberry Finn, The Red Badge of Courage, The Sound and the Fury, The Sun Also Rises,* or the poems of Frost, Eliot, and Stevens, the recommendations of *Democratic Vistas* are clearly out of touch with the American literary spirit. It is only such a work as Frank Norris's *The Octopus* that fulfills Whitman's specifications, and it is a pretty piece of irony that in that novel Presley, the would-be bard who speaks for Norris and wants to celebrate the expanding West in a rhapsodic poem, has apparently never heard of Whitman and delights in the idea that he may be known as the greatest American poet since Bryant.

One must notice that although Whitman speaks of "real literature" and wants a literary response to the realities of American life, he is certainly not demanding what since Stephen Crane and Howells we have been calling "realism" and "naturalism." And although there is a vigorous reforming note in his prophecy and although a connection is made between the People and literature, he is very far from urging "social realism," let alone "socialist realism" or "proletarian literature." At one point he actually urges writers to confront and oppose "the growing excess and arrogance of realism"; to be sure, he is not speaking technically of "literary realism," but the remark is encompassing enough to be relevant. And elsewhere he urges "no useless attempt to repeat the material creation, by daguerreotyping the exact likeness." It is thus only by example and in the limited ways we have noted above, in speaking of *Drum-Taps* [i.e., pp. 128–38 of *Walt Whitman Reconsidered*], that Whitman is a genuine precursor of modern realism.

Whitman of course asks too much of literature, as he does of "personalism," when he seems to hope that it can resolve the contradictions of democracy by furnishing archetypal images of perfect democratic persons and exploring the modes of human community. The literatus of democratic times, he says, has an even higher calling than the epic poet and prophet of "feudal" times. His task is harder because not only must he create the mythic archetypes of democracy—to take the place of Adam and Eve, Moses, Achilles, Prometheus, Arthur, Milton's Satan, Don Quixote, Shakespeare's Hamlet, Richard II, and Lear; he must also furnish all the spiritual guidance formerly provided by priests. We do know, to be sure, that Shelley's idea about poets being the unacknowledged legislators of the world is not mere illusion. Literature, even when it is abstruse and difficult, as Whitman's poetry often is, has its ways of entering into the national mind, a national mind like our own—at once so unformed and so Alexandrian—not excepted. And we know that the shape and emphasis of political institutions are determined by shared, unconscious patterns of thought. The great writer has his effect on these, even if he is so little read as Walt Whitman. But the fact remains that the "literatus" who creates democratic archetypes as Whitman speaks of them has turned out to be someone like Stephen Vincent

Benét—whose archetypes are synthetic products unhappily similar to the other products of our merchandising culture.

The most that can be said in defense of Whitman's program for literature is that literature does in truth deal with and exhibit modes of human community other than the mere idea of equality, which had always been the theoretical basis of Whitman's "adhesive" love of comrades. In *Democratic Vistas,* he had come to fear that equality was producing vulgarity and timidity, and that "a sort of dry and flat Sahara" was appearing in the midst of what ideally should be a various and energetic society. It is to Whitman's credit first, that he saw this to be true and, second, that he was not content merely to urge, as a cure, a more exalted equality. He does not, of course, abandon his faith in equality. He turns elsewhere in an attempt to understand how human experience may be shared and community formed without reducing life to a faceless uniformity. If we wish he had posited a vigorous, various, but harmonious political order, we must nevertheless observe that he was not entirely amiss in looking to literature, part of whose special prowess it is to seek out the difficult grounds of human commonalty.

Democratic Vistas impresses the reader with its many defects before it convinces him that it overcomes them. The piece is ill-organized and sometimes otiose. The language burgeons outrageously. One can decipher and accept a reference to nature's "kosmical, antiseptic power" or to history as a series of "idiocratic transfers." But there isn't much excuse for saying of "the third stage" of American history (the first is the laying of the political foundations, the second the consolidation of material progress) that "rising out of the previous ones, to make them and all illustrious, I, now, for one, promulge, announcing a native expression-spirit, getting into form, adult, and through mentality, for these States, self-contain'd, different from others, more expansive," and so on. There is less positively brilliant writing in *Democratic Vistas* than there is in the Preface of 1855, less that is in its way immediately authentic and final. At the same time the *Vistas* makes a more extensive use of the specific virtues of prose than does the Preface, and it has consequently a sustained polemical eloquence and the amplitude of effect and incident which are proper to a meditative and summary as well as a prophetic piece in which the author is reflecting on problems that have occupied a lifetime. There is great eloquence in the passages deploring America's "hollowness of heart"; a sharp satirical pleasure in the author's attacks on "flippancy, tepid amours, weak infidelism, small aims"; the old ability to catalogue the multifarious aspects of the city in such a way that the catalogue becomes a vision. And there are spiritedness and clairvoyance in what is doubtless the most valuable function of *Democratic Vistas*—its assertion of "the fresh, eternal qualities of Being."

There is much surface disorder in the loose and impassioned argument of Whitman's essay. Yet this seems a minor fault. Indeed, from a modern point of view, one may feel that a graver fault is the lack of an adequate sense of disorder. Like much amateur philosophy and much nineteenth-century social polemic *Democratic Vistas* strikes the modern reader as being too simply and schematically reasoned, as having underneath its surface sense of wildness, indeterminacy, and doubt a too simple, even a complacent, faith in the rational unities of democratic society, which in practice meant a too simple faith in the status quo. History, insofar as it is present at all, is regarded as maternal and beneficent. It therefore has no hazards and can be counted on to foster democracy. "The distinguishing event of my time," as Whitman called the Civil War, conspired to turn his mind too exclusively to modes of reconciliation, comradeship, and unity, and partly as a consequence of the one supreme tragic crisis of our civilization, he failed, like most of his contemporaries, to conceive of radically disastrous historical crises and dilemmas. He knew that the life of the self, of the individual, might involve such crises. But he did not believe that the same might be true of the history of nations, at least not of America and the nations of the future.

Still *Democratic Vistas* is an admirable and characteristic diatribe. And if one is sorry that in it Whitman is unable to conceive the extreme crises of society, one is certain that no society would be tolerable whose citizens could not find refreshment in its buoyant democratic idealism.

Selected Bibliography

TEXTS

The definitive edition is the *Reader's Comprehensive Edition of Leaves of Grass,* ed. Harold W. Blodgett and Sculley Bradley (New York: New York University Press, 1965; also available in the Norton paperback series). Contains the text of Whitman's final 1891-92 edition, an illuminating introduction, the Prefaces, and extensive notes. (Part of the *Collected Writings,* discussed below.)

The *Inclusive Edition of Leaves of Grass,* ed. Emory Holloway (New York: Doubleday, 1926), contains variant readings as well as selected manuscript variants.

Readers wishing to examine four of the earlier editions of *Leaves of Grass* discussed in the Introduction and in essays in this collection, may now easily do so. A fine and inexpensive paperback *Facsimile of the First* [1855] *Edition* is soundly introduced by Richard Bridgman for the Chandler Facsimile Editions Series (San Francisco: Chandler, 1968), and fills the gap left by the long out-of-print facsimile of the first edition, edited by Clifton J. Furness (New York: Columbia University Press, 1939). A unique *Facsimile of the First Edition 1855* containing also the eight pages of mixed reviews (including three of Whitman's own anonymous rave reviews of *Leaves*) and prose excerpts, mentioned in the Introduction, is available in a beautiful and expensive format from the Eakins Press, New York. (Through an oversight, the Eakins Press dust jacket mentions only one of Whitman's three anonymous reviews; the three are from the *Brooklyn Daily Times,* the *United States Review,* and the *American Phrenological Journal.*)

Malcolm Cowley, *Walt Whitman's Leaves of Grass, His Original Edition,* reprints the text of the 1855 edition (this is not a facsimile) with an excellent introduction (New York: Viking Compass Books, 1959). Cowley believes that the first is the best of all the editions of *Leaves*. On the other hand, Roy Harvey Pearce, in his perceptive Introduction to the paperback *Leaves of Grass: Facsimile Edition of the 1860* [Third Edition] *Text* (Ithaca: Cornell University Press, 1961), makes his case for the third edition as Whitman's masterpiece. (Whitman of course preferred the final 1891–92 edition and emphatically said so.) A facsimile of *Drum-Taps (1865) and Sequel to Drum-Taps (1865–66)* is introduced by F. DeWolfe Miller (Gainesville: Scholars Facsimiles and Reprints, 1959).

Also, a facsimile edition of the 120-page *Passage to India* volume (1871) is published by Haskell House (New York, 1969); the 1871 *Democratic Vistas* by Scholarly Press (St. Clair Shores, Michigan, 1970).

The growth of *Leaves of Grass* during formative periods of Whitman's career is detailed in *An 1855–56 Notebook Toward the Second Edition of Leaves of Grass,* ed. Harold W. Blodgett (Carbondale: Southern Illinois University Press, 1959); *Whitman's Manuscripts: Leaves of Grass (1860), A Parallel Text,* ed. Fredson Bowers (Chicago: University of Chicago Press, 1955); and *Walt Whitman's Blue Book,* 2 vols., ed. Arthur Golden (New York: New York Public Library, 1968).

Important collections of Whitman material are *Walt Whitman's Workshop,* ed. Clifton J. Furness (Cambridge: Harvard University Press, 1928); *Faint Clues and Indirections: Manuscripts of Walt Whitman and His Family,* ed. Clarence Gohdes and Rollo G. Silver (Durham: Duke University Press, 1949); and *Uncollected Poetry and Prose of Walt Whitman,* 2 vols., ed. Emory Holloway (New York: Doubleday, Page, 1921).

The *Collected Writings,* in progress (New York University Press), will make available in definitive editions the entire range of Whitman's poetry and prose. In addition to the *Reader's Comprehensive Edition of Leaves of Grass,* the following have been published so far: *The Early Poems and the Fiction,* ed. Thomas L. Brasher (1963); *Prose Works,* I, *Specimen Days* (1963) and II, *Collect and Other Prose* (1964), ed. Floyd Stovall; and the *Correspondence,* 5 vols. ed. Edwin Haviland Miller (1961–69). Forthcoming: the Variorum Edition of *Leaves of Grass,* the Notebooks, Diaries, Journalism, a Bibliography, and Miscellany. The *Collected Writings* will supersede the *Complete Writings,* 10 vols., ed. by the Literary Executors (1902). Despite its title, *Complete Writings* is far from being complete.

BIBLIOGRAPHIES

Current listings are found annually in *PMLA,* and quarterly in the *Walt Whitman Review* (which contains the most complete listings, from 1956 on) and *American Literature.* For 1970— *PMLA* also provides *Abstracts* of current scholarship, prepared by the authors. See also the important *Articles on American Literature, 1900–1950* (1951) and *1950–1967* (1970), ed. Lewis Leary (Durham: Duke University Press).

For critical bibliographies, see *Literary History of the United States,* ed. Robert Spiller, *et al.,* (New York: Macmillan, 1948; rev. 3rd ed., 1963, with Supplement); Willard Thorp, "Whitman," in *Eight American Authors,* ed. Floyd Stovall (New York: Modern Language Association, 1956; repr. with Supplement by J. Chesley Matthews, Norton paperback, 1963); Roger Asselineau, "Whitman [to 1970]," in *Eight American Authors: Revised Edition,* ed. James Woodress (New York: Norton, 1971); and *American Literary Scholarship: An Annual, 1963-67,* ed. James Woodress, and *1968–,* ed. J. Albert Robbins (Durham: Duke University Press). See also *The Year's Work in English Studies.*

BIOGRAPHICAL AND CRITICAL STUDIES

Allen, Gay Wilson. *The Solitary Singer: A Critical Biography of Walt Whitman* (New York: Macmillan, 1955; rev. New York University Press, 1967). The definitive biography.

———. *Walt Whitman Handbook* (Chicago, Packard and Co., 1946). This indispensable work covers in detail the various editions of *Leaves of Grass,* biographical approaches to the poet, his ideas, and his world-wide reputation.

———. *A Reader's Guide to Walt Whitman* (New York: Farrar, Straus & Giroux, 1970). Intended as "an introduction to intelligent reading and study of Whitman," this work brings up to date a number of points raised in the *Handbook.* (A selection is reprinted above.)

———. *Walt Whitman as Man, Poet, and Legend. With a Check List of Whitman Publications, 1945–1960* by Evie Allison Allen (Carbondale: Southern Illinois University Press, 1961). A collection of essays by the leading Whitman scholar, one of which, "Mutations in Whitman's Art," is reprinted above.

Arvin, Newton. *Whitman* (New York: Macmillan, 1938). Arvin focuses on Whitman and politics and science in this outstanding work.

Asselineau, Roger. *The Evolution of Walt Whitman:* I, *The Development of a Personality* and II, *The Creation of a Book* (Cambridge: Harvard University Press, 1960; 1962). A penetrating study of the man and his work by a leading French critic. Vol. II is especially good; a selection is reprinted above.

Bradley, Sculley. "The Fundamental Metrical Principle in Whitman's Poetry," *American Literature,* 10 (January 1939), 437–59. An illuminating analysis of Whitman's prosody.

Brasher, Thomas L. *Whitman as Editor of the Brooklyn Daily Eagle* (Detroit: Wayne State University Press, 1970). A sound study of an important phase of Whitman's career as journalist.

Chari, V. K. *Walt Whitman in the Light of Vedantic Mysticism* (Lincoln: University of Nebraska Press, 1964). A comparative analysis of Whitman's poetry and Indian literature.

Chase, Richard. *Walt Whitman Reconsidered.* (New York: Sloan Associates, 1955). A lively, critically acute study; one of the best around. A selection is reprinted above.

Coffman, Jr., Stanley K. "'Crossing Brooklyn Ferry': A Note on the Catalogue Technique in Whitman's Poetry," *Modern Philology,* 51 (May 1954), 225–32. Reprinted above.

———. "Form and Meaning in Whitman's 'Passage to India,'" *PMLA,* 70 (June 1955), 337–49. Though mainly favorable to the poem, Coffman makes an important contribution with his discussion of Whitman's confused treatment of the past in relation to the present in "Passage to India."

Faner, Robert D. *Walt Whitman and Opera* (Philadelphia: University of Pennsylvania Press, 1951). A full treatment of the subject.

Golden, Arthur. "New Light on *Leaves of Grass:* Whitman's Annotated Copy of the 1860 (Third) Edition," *Bulletin of the New York Public Library,* 69 (May 1965), 283–306. The impact of the Civil War on Whitman's revisions for *Leaves of Grass,* with emphasis on nationalistic poetry, "Children of Adam," and "Calamus." (Reprinted above.)

Hindus, Milton, ed. *Leaves of Grass One Hundred Years After* (Palo Alto: Stanford University Press, 1955). Essays by William Carlos Williams, Richard Chase, Kenneth Burke, Leslie A. Fiedler, David Daiches, and J. Middleton Murry, with those by Williams, Chase, and Burke of special interest.

————, ed. *Walt Whitman: The Critical Heritage* (London: Routledge & Kegan Paul, 1971). A fine collection of essays from 1855 to 1914.

Holloway, Emory. *Whitman: An Interpretation in Narrative* (New York: Knopf, 1926). Though superseded by Allen's *Solitary Singer,* contains many acute observations on the poet and his times, despite Holloway's lapse on Whitman's fanciful early romance in New Orleans with a Creole lady.

Hungerford, Edward. "Walt Whitman and His Chart of Bumps," *American Literature,* 2 (January 1931), 350-84. A detailed analysis of Whitman's interest in phrenology.

Jannacone, Pasquale. *Walt Whitman's Poetry and the Evolution of Rhythmic Forms* and *Walt Whitman's Thought and Art,* trans. Peter Mitilineos (Washington, D.C.: Microcard Editions, 1973). This important work on Whitman's poetic technique is accompanied by a short essay by Jannacone.

Jarrell, Randall. "Some Lines from Whitman," in *Poetry and the Age* (New York: Knopf, 1953). A sensitive essay on Whitman and his poetry by a first-rate poet in his own right.

Lewis, R. W. B. *The American Adam: Innocence, Tragedy, and Tradition in the Nineteenth Century* (Chicago: University of Chicago Press, 1955). This important work contains a sensitive account of Whitman as the "New Adam."

————, ed. *The Presence of Walt Whitman: Selected Papers from the English Institute* (New York: Columbia University Press, 1962). A stimulating, far-ranging collection of essays.

Matthiessen, F. O. *American Renaissance: Art and Expression in the Age of Emerson and Whitman* (New York: Oxford University Press, 1941). In this classic study, Matthiessen offers incisive analyses of the art of Emerson, Thoreau, Whitman, Hawthorne, and Melville.

Miller, Edwin Haviland. *Walt Whitman's Poetry: A Psychological Journey* (Boston: Houghton Mifflin, 1968). Overall, a penetrating psychological study of Whitman's major poetry, marred at times by Miller's rejection of "external" (textual) evidence in favor of a strictly psychological approach. (A section is reprinted above.)

————, ed. *A Century of Whitman Criticism* (Bloomington: Indiana University Press, 1970). This comprehensive collection of essays is soundly introduced.

Miller, Jr., James E. *A Critical Guide to Leaves of Grass* (Chicago: University of Chicago Press, 1957). At times Miller overdoes his insistence on the "mystical" Whitman, but in the main a sound study.

———, Karl Shapiro, and Bernice Slote. *Start with the Sun: Studies in the Whitman Tradition* (Lincoln: University of Nebraska Press, 1960). Stimulating essays, round-robin style, on Whitman's influence on, among others, D. H. Lawrence, Hart Crane, and Dylan Thomas. An essay by Miller is reprinted above.

Murphy, Francis, ed. *Walt Whitman: A Critical Anthology* (Baltimore: Penguin Books, 1970). A comprehensive collection of essays on Whitman, including contemporary critical estimates to those of the present.

Pearce, Roy Harvey. *The Continuity of American Poetry* (Princeton: Princeton University Press, 1961). A perceptive account of the development of American poetry from the seventeenth century to the present.

———, ed. *Whitman: A Collection of Critical Essays* (Englewood Cliffs, N.J.: Prentice Hall, 1962). A sound collection of essays.

Schyberg, Frederik. *Walt Whitman,* trans. from the Danish by Evie Allison Allen (New York: Columbia University Press, 1951). Biographical details of the poet used convincingly to illuminate Schyberg's analysis of the various editions of *Leaves of Grass.*

Spitzer, Leo. *"Explication de texte* Applied to Walt Whitman's Poem 'Out of the Cradle Endlessly Rocking,'" *ELH: A Journal of English Literary History,* 16 (September 1949), 229–49. A sensitive reading of one of Whitman's major poems.

Tanner, Tony. *The Reign of Wonder: Naivety and Reality in American Literature* (Cambridge, England: Cambridge University Press, 1965; repr. Harper paperback, 1967). Main emphasis in this fresh study is on nineteenth-century American literature as the expression of an immediate and concrete directness of experience.

Weathers, Willie T. "Whitman's Poetic Translations of His 1855 Preface," *American Literature,* 19 (March 1947), 21–40. How Whitman turned poetry in essay form into poetry in stanzaic form, with special attention to the nationalistic poem "By Blue Ontario's Shore."

Whicher, Stephen E. "Whitman's Awakening to Death: Toward a Biographical Reading of 'Out of the Cradle Endlessly Rocking,'" *Studies in Romanticism,* 1 (Autumn 1961), 9–28. A sensitive approach to an important phase of Whitman's career. (Reprinted above.)